fine Gardening

GROW

HEALTHIER & EASIER GARDENS

fine Gardening

GROW

HEALTHIER & EASIER GARDENS

698 TIPS and TECHNIQUES

Editors, Contributors & Readers of *Fine Gardening*

The Taunton Press

The Taunton Press
Inspiration for hands-on living®

The Taunton Press, Inc.
63 South Main Street
PO Box 5506
Newtown, CT 06470-5506
e-mail: tp@taunton.com

Executive editor: Shawna Mullen
Assistant editor: Tim Stobierski
Developmental editor: Nanette Maxim
Copy editor: Valerie Cimino
Indexer: Barbara Mortenson
Cover and Interior design: carol singer | notice design
Layout coordinator: Amy Griffin
Layout: Kimberly Shake
Cover photographer: Carole Drake/GAP Photos; Garden design: Phillipa Lambert

The following names/manufacturers appearing in *Fine Gardening Grow* are
trademarks: AstroTurf®, Autumn Radiance®, Bitrex®, Black Lace™, Bobbex™, Bonide®,
Bravo®, Bulb Booster®, Daconil®, Deer Off®, Deer Stopper®, Dithane™, Gardens Alive!®,
Heritage®, Hint of Gold™, Ivory®, Milorganite®, Murphy®, Plantskydd®, Raspberry
Delight®, Roundup®, Soap-Shield®, Subdue®, Tiger Eyes™, Vapor Gard®

Library of Congress Cataloging-in-Publication Data
Fine gardening grow healthier & easier gardens : 698 gardening tips and techniques /
editors of Fine gardening.
    pages cm
  Other title: Grow healthier and easier gardens
  Other title: 698 gardening tips and techniques
  Includes index.
  ISBN 978-1-62710-795-2
1. Gardening. I. Fine gardening. II. Title: Grow healthier and easier gardens. III. Title:
698 gardening tips and techniques.
  SB450.97.F56 2015
  635--dc23
                    2014042054

Printed in the United States of America
10 9 8 7 6 5 4 3 2 1

CONTENTS

ACKNOWLEDGMENTS

Special thanks to the readers, authors, editors, copy editors, and other staff members of *Fine Gardening* and The Taunton Press books department who contributed to the making of this book.

INTRODUCTION

Information presented in these small bites is easier to remember when you need it most: when you are out in the garden or at the nursery.

When speaking with the experts who contribute the content to *Fine Gardening*, the conversation invariably turns to the issues I am facing in my own garden. A discussion of the proper way to prune crape myrtles quickly becomes a conversation about the best way to deal with the unruly lilac at the edge of my driveway. It's only natural to want to learn more about what you are doing from someone who knows volumes more than you do, so I get as much as I can out of every chat. These talks have yielded great results, helping me to make my garden healthier, lusher, and greener. And when my plants do die, at least I know what I did to kill them.

Collected here for the first time are favorite tips, tricks, shortcuts, and gardening know-how from the experts who contribute to *Fine Gardening*. You can follow the advice the leaders in the fields of gardening, horticulture, garden design, and soil science have given to me—and to all of the readers of *Fine Gardening*.

This book collects all of the best gardening tips from the *Fine Gardening* archive and divides up into an easy-to-use, quick reference format that functions as a helpful partner to watch over your shoulder as you prep your soil, start your seeds, divide your perennials, prune your shrubs, and harvest your veggies. Information presented in these small bites is easier to remember when you need it most: when you are out in the garden or at the nursery.

Armed with such knowledge, is there any reason why you should not be able to manage your soil, cultivate your crops, design your beds, control your pests, and enjoy your garden as well as other expert gardeners? I think you will find that if you follow the collective wisdom of these experts, you will, without a doubt, be thrilled with improvements made to your garden. No matter how you look at it, the results will be stunning.

—Steve Aitken

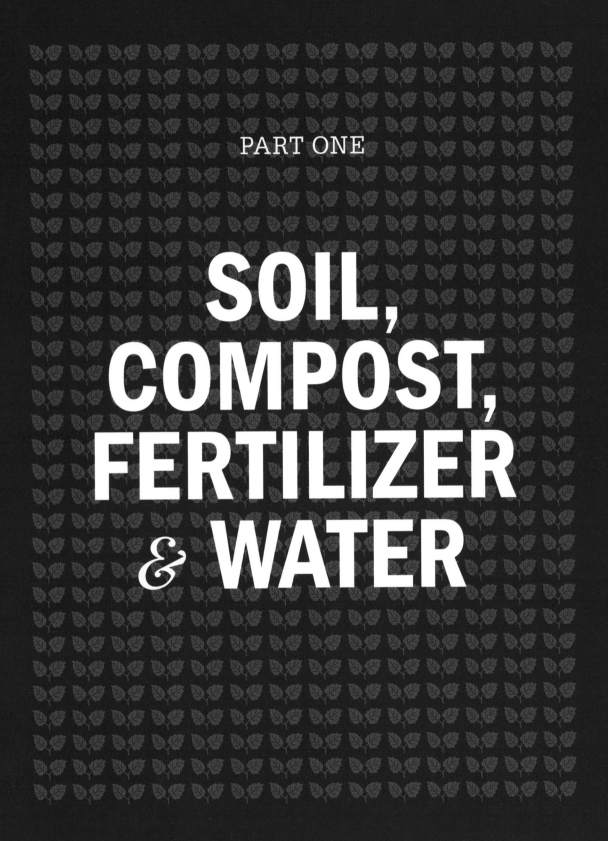

PART ONE

SOIL, COMPOST, FERTILIZER & WATER

SOIL

GET TO KNOW YOUR SOIL

Investigate Your Soil

—JOHN BRAY

Dig into your garden and find out whether you have clay or sandy soil; it makes a big difference in your drainage. Clay-laden soil presents special watering challenges. Clay has an electrical charge that draws water, pulling it away from plant roots. In dense clay, little room exists for passages that permit the exchange of essential gases with the air aboveground. Clay soil also drains slowly. Water flows more easily through sandy soil; but if it's too sandy, water may leach out too quickly and take dissolved nutrients with it. Both clay and sandy soils can be turned into a preferred loam by mixing in organic material, such as compost.

DO A HAND-TEXTURING TEST

A hand-texturing test is one method of determining the texture of your soil. How long is your ribbon? To determine the texture of your soil, measure the ribbon.

- If your ribbon measures less than 1 inch long before breaking, you have loam or silt.

- If your ribbon measures 1 to 2 inches long before breaking, you have clay loam.

- If your ribbon measures more than 2 inches long before breaking, you have clay.

—LEE REICH

Add water to a small amount of dry soil, and form it into a ball if you can.

Knead the soil between your fingers to form a flat ribbon.

SOIL pH

Every plant has its preferred range of acidity, from 0 to 14 on the pH scale—7 is neutral, and as numbers decrease the acidity gets higher; as the numbers increase from 7, so does the alkalinity. Most cultivated plants enjoy slightly acidic conditions with a pH of about 6.5. Pin oak, gardenia, blueberry, azalea, and rhododendron are among the plants that demand a very acidic pH of 4.5 to 5.5. Most plants thrive in slightly acidic soil because that pH affords them good access to all nutrients. Earthworms thrive in slightly acidic soil, too, as well as microorganisms that convert nitrogen into forms that plants can use.

—LEE REICH

Test Your Soil's pH

Always test your soil to know its current pH level before attempting to change it. A simple soil test can be done at home or by a soil-testing laboratory. You must also know your soil's texture, be it clay, sand, or something in between. More material is needed to change the pH level of a clay soil than that of a sandy soil because the charged surfaces of clays make them more resistant to pH changes than the uncharged surfaces of sand particles.

Use Limestone to Raise pH and Sulfur to Lower It

Generally, limestone is used to raise a pH level. Limestone is relatively pure calcium carbonate, but dolomitic limestone is a mix of calcium carbonate and magnesium. Pound for pound, dolomitic limestone neutralizes more acidity than pure limestone and adds magnesium to the soil, perfect for those who garden in the East or the Pacific Northwest, where this nutrient is naturally low. Sulfur will lower a pH level.

Choose Pellets Over the Powdered Form of Limestone or Sulfur

Both are available in powdered or pelletized form, the latter being easier to spread uniformly and causing less of a health hazard from dust. Neither is water-soluble, so mix these materials thoroughly into the top 6 inches of soil when quick action is needed. Otherwise, just lay the material on top of the ground and let it work its way down. Make sure to monitor the pH regularly—the soil can shift because of the presence of elements such as minerals and fertilizer use.

WEAVE THE SOIL FOOD WEB

Soil is composed of minerals, which make up the nonliving portion, and the food web, which includes minute creatures, also called soil biota, that bring the soil to life. Improving soil tilth, texture, aeration, drainage, and nutritional content by feeding the garden compost and other amendments tips the scales toward helpful soil biota.

—ANN LOVEJOY

Bring on the Nitrogen-Fixing Bacteria

These bacteria dine on particles of humus (organic matter), creating a waste product called bacteria manure that adds new forms of organic content to soil. Many plants absorb nutrients most efficiently through this bacterial waste product, so the more nitrogen-fixing bacteria in the soil, the better. Lawns, flower beds, and most vegetables will flourish in soils dominated by beneficial bacteria.

Let Earthworms Wriggle

Among the most beneficial of soil dwellers, earthworms tunnel through heavy soil to let air get down to plant roots. Additionally, their castings promote sturdy root growth and feed many soil dwellers.

Know Good Fungi from Bad

Most gardeners assume that fungi must be bad for the soil, but this is far from the truth. Fungi are vitally important to soil health, and beneficial forms are found in virtually every kind of soil on earth. Mycorrhizae are among the best-known fungi. They attach themselves to the roots of plants and create a mesh of fine feeder "rootlets" that act like pumps, pulling nutrients and water into the host plant's root system.

Let Arthropods Play Soil Traffic Cop

These recyclers are the critters that feed on bacteria, fungi, and earthworms as well as plant particles. They include microarthropods—very small organisms like mites—and larger organisms like sow bugs, springtails, spiders, and centipedes. The microarthropods stay put in the soil, consuming debris and making nitrogen and other nutrients more readily available to plants and other soil biota. Arthropods also control the population levels of other organisms in the soil, keeping it balanced naturally.

Not All Nematodes Are No-Nos

Nematodes, like fungi, are usually assumed to be pathogens, but beneficial nematodes abound in the soil. Good garden soil contains an ample supply of beneficial nematodes, which feed on many other creatures, from bacteria and protozoa to other nematodes, including the pathogenic ones. Beneficial nematodes support root growth, passing vital nutrients along to plants through their manure. Pathogenic nematodes eat live plant tissue, harming root growth. In healthy soil, beneficial nematodes help to keep their pathogenic cousins under control.

Protozoa Are Pals

Soil-dwelling protozoa are single-celled organisms that eat bacteria, keeping the bad bacteria in check, and produce a manure rich in available nitrogen, which can be taken up by plants. Protozoa are a favored food for nematodes and other soil fauna, which, in turn, release nitrogen and other nutrients back into the soil as they excrete.

SOIL TERMS YOU NEED TO KNOW

Good gardens start from the ground up, so an understanding of some basic terms will help you build the best soil for your plants.

Texture

Texture describes nothing more than the size ranges of the mineral particles that make up a particular soil. Those size ranges are defined in three broad classes: Clay is the smallest, silt is a bit bigger, and sand has the largest particles. Texture is important because the sizes of particles reflect the sizes of the pore spaces between them, which, in turn, influences the amount of air and water (held by capillary attraction) the soil can hold. Rare is the garden soil that is pure sand, silt, or clay, so textures usually have such names as *sandy clay* or *silty clay* to indicate a particular mix. A soil with roughly equal functional contributions from clay, silt, and sand is texturally a *loam*. Plants generally like loamy soils because the variety of particle sizes provides for a good balance of air and water in the soil.

Structure

Structure refers to the crystalline units formed by soil particles clumping together. A clay soil might have insufficient air because its many small pores cling to capillary water. It is possible, however, to have a clay soil with good structure, one where plenty of air is held in the pore spaces that exist between larger aggregates.

Friability and Tilth

Friability and tilth, while not exactly the same thing, are closely related from a plant's point of view. A soil that is friable crumbles rather than wads up when you squeeze it gently in your hand. Tilth is the physical condition of the soil as far as plants are concerned, and a soil that is friable is in good tilth. Good structure puts a soil in good tilth.

Cultivation

Cultivation, in the world of gardening, has more than one meaning. One sense is to stir the soil, such as you might do with your hoe or your rototiller. Such cultivation kills weed seedlings and loosens the soil surface so that water more readily percolates. Cultivate also means to care for plants in a more general sense. Cultivating the soil—keeping it in good tilth—is one component of cultivating plants.

Well-Drained Soil

Soil that is well drained allows water to readily percolate through it, affording roots plenty of air. Drainage is related to both texture and structure: Sandy soils generally have little structure but, with large pores, are well drained (often too much so, not holding sufficient water); clay soils, at the other extreme, are well drained only if they have good structure and thus are in good tilth. (See "Investigate Your Soil," p. 7.)

Organic Matter

Organic matter is the living and once living component of the soil. The low percentage of organic matter in soils—usually only a few percent—doesn't reflect its importance. Besides its positive influence on plant nutrition and health, organic matter also provides the glues that lead to good structure (and, hence, friability), good drainage, and good tilth.

—LEE REICH

SOIL AMENDMENTS

Getting the most out of your soil starts with what you put into it. From organic matter to Epsom salts to alfalfa meal, here's what you need to know to get the most out of your dirt.

—LEE REICH

Have a Good Sense of Humus

Humus is what's left after organic materials are added to the soil and the fraction of these materials that decomposes most readily has done so. What remains is a witch's brew of stuff that constitutes only a small percentage of the soil but has a profound and beneficial effect on plant nutrition. During its slow decomposition, this dark brown material releases nutrients, especially nitrogen, into the soil. It renders nutrients already in the soil more available to plants and prevents nutrients such as calcium and potassium from washing through the soil beyond the reach of plant roots. Another benefit of humus comes from its acting like glue, cementing soil particles together into aggregates. Such aggregates are less subject to erosion and create a range of pore sizes, which lets air and water move freely into and within the soil even as the humus itself sponges up water to hold for plant use.

TWO WAYS TO ADD HUMUS

Let organic material on the ground decay naturally.
PRO: Humus lasts longer.
CON: Humus is not immediately available.

Till the organic matter into the soil.
PRO: Humus is available quickly.
CON: Humus is soon burned up and needs replenishing.

Work Compost Into New Beds

During the initial, pre-garden phase of a soil-improvement plan, break up 10 inches of hard-packed clay with a mattock. Spread compost over the surface of the beds 1 inch at a time and rototill it in, being careful not to work the clay when it is too wet, because clay worked wet can result in some tenacious clods, very reluctant in their willingness to ever come apart again. Try to work the compost deep into the soil. Incorporation to ample depth is very important to permit roots to grow into the subsoil.

Mulch With Organic Materials

It's important not to burn the humus up faster than it's added, which would be akin to withdrawing more money from your bank account than you deposit. Mulching with organic materials, rather than digging them in, is a more effective way to increase soil humus, especially in already well-aerated sandy soils.

Epsom Salts May Help Your Roses

Ever hear the story about the little old lady who grows prizewinning roses by sprinkling the ground beneath them with Epsom salts? The question is: Should we follow her lead? Not necessarily. Epsom salts are not magic; they are magnesium sulfate, a source of the plant foods magnesium and sulfur. If your soil lacks either, Epsom salts will give your plants a boost; if not, the effect will be nil or negative.

Alfalfa Meal Is a Natural Source for Nitrogen

Ground alfalfa leaves and stems create alfalfa meal. As a legume, the alfalfa plant absorbs nitrogen from the air. Thus, its foliage is a significant source of nitrogen when added to the soil. As the meal decomposes, it releases nitrogen as well as smaller quantities of phosphorous, potassium, and micronutrients. Plus, alfalfa contains the plant hormone triacontanol, which can boost plant growth.

NUTRITIONAL FIXES

Soybean Meal Provides Nitrogen

Nitrogen is the third major plant nutrient (in addition to potassium and phosphorous), and soybean meal is often specifically recommended as a way to supply it to plants needing acidic soils. In such soils, the breakdown of raw soybean meal into usable nitrogen proceeds only to the point of putting it in a form enjoyed by plants. It can be used to feed any plant, and it does so in sync with plant growth, so one feeding can last the whole season. Be careful, though: Used excessively, soybean meal can burn roots, overstimulate plant growth, and take on the aroma of a dead animal.

Gypsym Amps Up the Calcium

A mined mineral that is nothing more than calcium sulfate (plaster of Paris), gypsum may not supply plants with nutrients calcium and sulfur, but when applied to clay soils high in sodium, it improves drainage. The calcium in gypsum displaces the sodium, allowing the clay particles to clump together into larger units through which the water more readily drains. Because gypsum has no effect on soil pH, it can supply calcium with no change in acidity.

Add Rock Phosphate for Slow-Release Phosphorus

Rock phosphate is a naturally mined mineral that supplies phosphorus, another major plant nutrient. You can find rock phosphate in three forms: colloidal phosphate, soft rock phosphate, and hard rock phosphate. These minerals contain micronutrients and release a small percentage of their phosphorus each year.

Sprinkle Wood Ashes to Boost Potassium

If you have off-color leaves (browning around the edges), your soil may lack potassium. Rather than reach for a bag of 10-10-10, which is 10 percent potassium, spread wood ashes. Depending on the kind of wood burned, wood ashes contain 3 to 7 percent potassium, plus an array of other nutrients in lesser amounts. Wood ashes, however, also decrease soil acidity. If over-applied (more than 20 pounds per thousand square feet), they can be detrimental for some plants. Don't sprinkle the ashes beneath rhododendrons, blueberries, or other plants that require acidic soil.

—LEE REICH

Myth: Add Sand to Loosen Heavy Clay Soil

—JOHN C. FECH

The worst remedy for a clay soil is to add sand. This practice turns the clay soil into a rock-hard, mortarlike substance. Instead, use organic matter, like compost, to loosen heavy soils because it is light in composition and also improves nutrient quality. Sand can improve a clay soil, but it must be added until it constitutes most of the mineral composition of the soil. At that point, it's not really clay soil any longer; it is sandy soil.

Dump On the Compost

—KEITH BALDWIN

Composts are integral to a clay soil management plan. Because of the humified nature of compost and its low concentrations of oxidizable carbon and available nitrogen, compost is relatively resistant to further decomposition, and additions of compost to the soil over time can increase the soil's organic carbon and humic matter content. Add compost not so much to provide nutrients as to provide stabilized organic matter that will improve the physical properties of the soil.

Prevent Frost Heaves

—FINE GARDENING EDITORS

Cycles of freezing and thawing of the soil can sometimes push shallow-rooted plants out of the ground. Once the roots are exposed to the harsh winter elements, the plant is in danger of dying; heucheras and ornamental grasses are particularly susceptible to this winter phenomenon. A thick layer of mulch is the key to avoiding frost heaves. The extra layer works like a blanket and helps regulate the soil temperature.

Frost heave damage

Add Organic Materials to the Soil
—LEE REICH

The most obvious way to create humus is to add organic materials—living or once-living materials such as manure, straw, or leaves—to the soil, either digging them into the soil or laying them on the surface as mulch. Don't dig organic materials too deeply into the soil, though, for they function most efficiently in the best-aerated and most biologically active layers of the soil, which are near the surface. Merely growing plants also adds humus, as their dead portions join the soil and begin to decay.

Plant Cover Crops During Fallow Periods
—KEITH BALDWIN

A strategy for adding organic matter to clay soil is cover cropping. Plant cover crops any time the beds in your garden would otherwise be unplanted or fallow. Fallow periods provide little additional organic biomass while allowing the decomposition of organic matter in the soil to continue. Cover crops provide you with a variety of services. They contribute to improvements in soil structure. They reduce erosion and increase infiltration. And they can smother weeds and even suppress weed seed germination. Many cover crops will also suppress pathogenic nematodes, such as root knot nematode.

Choose Your Mulch
—FINE GARDENING EDITORS

A thick layer of mulch has a multitude of benefits, and it's the single most effective way to make your garden look neat and tidy. A 3- to 4-inch-deep layer of mulch—whether it is garden compost, well-composted manure, grass clippings, or shredded bark—will suppress weeds; regulate soil temperatures; conserve moisture; contribute nutrients to the soil; and lend a polished, manicured air to your garden beds. It's a no-brainer.

Use mulch to suppress weeds, regulate temperatures, conserve moisture, and feed plants.

Till Hard, Then Lightly

—KEITH BALDWIN

Although you want to work the soil hard before initial planting, major losses in soil organic matter content can take place when the soil is inverted or mixed annually by tillage. Extensive tillage stimulates microbial activity (gives the little guys an appetite, so to speak), and the consumption of mass quantities of organic matter ensues. After your clay soil becomes more friable and you have provided a deep root zone for your garden plants, you should consider reducing tillage. Switching to a minimum-till system increases soil organic matter, soil organic carbon, total nitrogen, and soil microbial biomass carbon and nitrogen content, especially at the surface and in the top 2 to 4 inches.

Apply Winter Mulch to Protect Perennials

—JEFF GILLMAN

Snow keeps plants underground at a temperature around freezing and protects them from the worst of winter conditions. If we could be sure that there would be a good layer of snow throughout winter, our gardens wouldn't experience many problems at all. Without snow or other mulch in tough winter months, however, plants may suffer heaving and freezing, which can damage their root systems.

The best time to apply winter mulch is just after the first hard frost. By putting mulch down at this time, you will help stabilize the temperature of the soil right around freezing. Applying mulch too soon may delay freezing and encourage heaving and thawing. Applying it too late may cause the roots of plants to experience temperatures below that which they can handle.

Pine bark or wood chips are the best mulches; they enrich soil as they degrade. A layer of mulch 4 to 6 inches deep over the plants works well. Most perennials will pop through the mulch in spring. If the plants are young, small, or newly planted in the fall, you may need to clear some of the mulch in the spring so that the plants can emerge without difficulty through the winter protection.

A Soil Thermometer Can Help You Plant at the Right Time

—BRANDI SPADE

Unless you're really good at guessing, chances are that you could use a soil thermometer. Warm-season crops will be stunted if planted when the soil is too cold, whereas cool-season crops need to reach maturity before the soil gets too warm and plants begin to bolt. Air temperature is not a good gauge of soil temperature. A soil thermometer can help you determine not only how soon to start your veggies (according to recommended temperatures listed on seed packets) but also how long you can extend the planting season into late summer and fall.

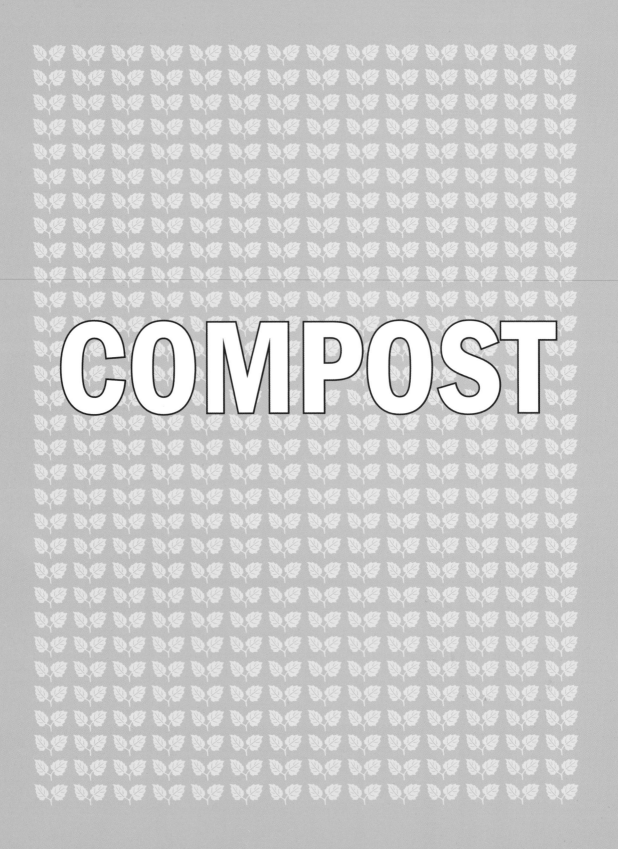

COMPOST

COMPOSTING 411

Keep Your Compost Odor-Free
—NANCY GIESE

The odor of compost is a common concern, but it shouldn't be. Good compost has an earthy aroma to it. If it has an offensive smell, like ammonia or sulfur, it is not "cooking" properly. In order for compost to cook properly, you need a good mix of heat, moisture, and oxygen in your pile so that bacteria and microorganisms can do their job.

Bacteria begin the composting process. Aerobic bacteria need air to live, while anaerobic bacteria can survive without it. Both aid in the decay of organic material, but the aerobic bacteria are particularly helpful because they work faster than their anaerobic cousins and do not produce an odor while working. If your compost pile begins to smell, that usually means that your aerobic friends are not getting enough oxygen. The solution? Get a pitchfork and turn your pile.

Let Your Composter Pull Double Duty as a Trellis
—JENNY BLACKWELL

To assemble a compost tower, simply nestle a column of chicken wire among plants, bury the bottom inch into the ground for stability, fill the tower with pulled weeds, and train your favorite viners to scramble up the sides. Towers can range from 2 to 8 feet tall by 6 inches to 3 feet wide. Continue adding garden debris all season, keeping a one-to-one ratio between carbon-rich and nitrogen-rich matter, and let the tower decompose all winter. By spring, you'll have rich compost at the bottom of each tower.

Skip the Diseased and the Chemically Treated
—NANCY GIESE

Diseased plants (dead or alive) shouldn't be composted because they can spread the disease further. If you have applied chemicals like herbicides or pesticides to your lawn, those grass clippings shouldn't be composted either. Perennial weeds, like dandelions, should be discarded as well.

Raised Beds Can Serve as Compost Bins

—JENNY BLACKWELL

Sheet mulching offers a way to fill raised beds with kitchen and garden waste instead of pricey bagged soil. To fill a bed, begin with a layer of woody cuttings chopped up into 1-inch-long pieces; this will ensure good drainage. Add a 4- to 8-inch-deep layer of straw or dried leaves, and water the bed. Spread a 1-inch-deep layer of well-rotted manure or compost; lay down a 4-inch-deep layer of kitchen scraps, weeds, or grass clippings; and add another fluffy layer of leaves or straw. Alternate layers of straw or leaves, compost, and green scraps until the bed is full. Water one last time, and let the bed decompose. After the bed has shrunk considerably, fill it up again with more layers of organic matter, top it off with a 6-inch-deep layer of soil, and plant. Heavy feeders, like tomatoes and peppers, love these nutrient-rich beds. To offset the nitrogen imbalance that can occur as organic matter decays, mix in an organic fertilizer, like fish emulsion or blood meal.

Layer for Speed

—NANCY GIESE

Most gardeners have heard about layering their compost: a layer of dry ingredients (usually leaves), then a layer of moist ingredients (grass clippings or kitchen peelings), and so on. In an ideal world, gardeners would have the time and the energy to layer their compost. Truth be told, Mother Nature and her workers have composted for millennia, and they have never layered. Admittedly, though, the process is faster if your ingredients are layered.

Go Green (Manure)

—JENNIFER BROWN

Green manures are not the by-products of animal waste. Rather, they are crops that are grown solely to be turned into the ground while they're still green. By doing this, you add a good dose of organic matter to the soil. Green manures are most useful in vegetable gardens where an entire area or bed can be sown and the growth can be turned under by hand or with a tiller. Using green manures in a new garden can be a great way to improve the soil before planting begins.

Green manures can be planted in all parts of the country and in any season. Most are quick growers, and some can be mixed into the soil less than two weeks after planting. During the warm times of the year, or in warmer climates, plants like hairy vetch, many kinds of clover and peas, and soybeans, oats, buckwheat, barley, or alfalfa can be used. During the winter months, especially in colder areas of the country, winter rye or wheat can be used. No matter which crop you choose, turn it before it goes to seed to keep the plants from self-sowing.

Sunshine Helps Make Compost
—NANCY GIESE

You can put your compost pile in the sun or in the shade, but putting it in the sun will hasten the composting process. Sun helps increase the temperature, so the bacteria and fungi work faster. This also means that your pile will dry out faster, especially in warm southern climates. If you do place your pile in full sun, just remember to keep it moist as it heats up.

CREATE GOOD COMPOST

Compost is made from the breakdown of organic material, with nonorganic material like minerals and sand added for texture. The heat generated kills any weed seeds and reduces vegetable matter to finer particles. The resulting "black gold"—a loose, odorless, rich source of nutrients—will greatly improve the quality of your soil and the health of the plants that live in it.

Add

Garden trimming and leaves

Dry leaves

Vegetable waste

Coffee grounds

Apple cores, banana peels, and citrus rinds

Rice

Pasta (and the sauce if it doesn't contain meat)

Salad greens (and the dressing if it's made from vegetable oil)

Breads

Avoid

Animal products, like meat, bones, or fats—they will rot and give off bad odors

Whole eggshells—crush them first to help them decompose

Shredded paper, except in small amounts and only if the paper doesn't have a lot of ink or color in it

Sawdust that is made from pressure-treated lumber

Anything that might be toxic to *you*

—FRED PAPPALARDO

Mushroom Compost Is an Earthy Alternative

—PAUL J. WUEST

Mushroom compost, sometimes called mushroom soil, is the spent growing medium used by commercial mushroom farmers. Commercial mushrooms grow in a specially formulated and processed compost made from wheat straw, hay, corncobs, cottonseed hulls, gypsum, and chicken manure.

When the mushroom harvest is finished, farmers steam-pasteurize everything in the growing room and dispose of the spent growing medium, often selling it to the gardening public. Mushroom compost is great for gardens as a mulch or as a slow-release fertilizer when mixed into soil. It has an NPK ratio of 2-1-1 and a pH of 6.8. The compost ingredients have very low levels of heavy metals, and mushroom farmers have used integrated pest management practices for decades, so they rarely use pesticides on mushroom crops. With the steam pasteurization, all weed seeds are killed in the mushroom compost, as are any insects or other pests that might be present.

Hot and Cold Composting

—LYNN BEMENT

Hot composting is faster but requires attention to keep carbon and nitrogen in the optimum ratio. Whether you want quick results or are content to let compost "happen" at its own speed, as in cold composting, there is a method for you. Either way, you'll get a terrific soil amendment for your garden.

Keys to Hot Composting

Temperatures rising in a hot-compost pile come from the activity of numerous organisms breaking down organic matter. To keep a pile running hot, pay attention to four elements: carbon, nitrogen, water, and air.

A hot pile requires enough high-nitrogen materials to get the pile to heat up. The ratio by volume should be 2 parts carbon to 1 part nitrogen. To aid in decomposition, keep the mixture as damp as a wrung-out sponge but not sopping wet. A variety of different-size materials (like twigs, stalks, straw, or hay) creates air pockets. You also increase the air-oxygen exchange every time you turn the pile.

If the pile is built correctly, it will heat up within 24 to 36 hours to the ideal temperature of 141°F to 155°F (weed seeds and disease pathogens die at these temperatures) and will maintain its temperature for several days to a week or longer. Use a compost thermometer to monitor the temperature. If the temperature starts to drop or if it gets hotter than 160°F, turn the pile again and add water. This should be done several times. A hot pile takes more effort but will produce compost more quickly—in several weeks to several months.

Keys to Cold Composting

Cold composting requires minimal effort but may take a year or two before it produces compost you can use in your garden.

This method of cold composting has two steps: Put your waste in a pile, and wait. You can think of cold composting as the add-as-you-have-materials pile. The time needed to have finished compost is hard to estimate because it depends on the materials in your pile and the size of the particles. The smaller the particles, the faster they will break down. Do not put in weeds that have gone to seed or diseased plants. Without high temperatures to kill off weed seeds or disease pathogens, you will be spreading these bad guys around your landscape.

WORM COMPOSTING

Get to Know Nature's
Ultimate Recyclers

—JOAN D. FILSINGER

Worms take garbage in and turn out black gold. To create a worm-composting haven in a bin, you can't use just any old worms. You need worms that are real chowhounds. Red wigglers, which are also called red worms, are the most voracious eaters of the earthworm family. They can consume half their own weight in organic matter each day and leave behind fertile compost. Pale red, the tiny, threadlike baby worms grow from ⅛ inch up to 4 inches long at maturity.

Red wigglers are available from garden-supply catalogs and through ads in gardening magazines. They are sold either by the number of worms or by the pound. Prices range from $20 to $40 per pound, which is usually about 1,000 worms. Since they won't survive shipping in cold weather, you may not be able to purchase them by mail from November through March. Start with 2 pounds of worms for a two- or three-person household.

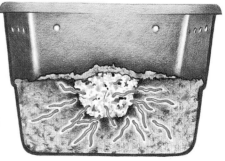

Bury food scraps in the bedding, and let the worms come wriggling. Holes near the top of a worm bin let in air, and bottom holes let excess water drain out.

Create a Cozy Home for Your Worms
—JOAN D. FILSINGER

These wigglers are in worm heaven as long as you give them a dark, cozy home with plenty of food, moisture, oxygen, and a comfortable temperature (from 50°F to 70°F). You won't have to worry about them escaping from their bin as long as you provide the right conditions.

Worms are photophobic—they shun both sun and artificial light, burrowing as deep as they can. Use a dark-colored bin, or drape it with a dark covering. If you move the worm bin outside in warmer weather, make sure it stays covered in a cool, shaded place.

Worm bins are commercially available, but they can be expensive—from $50 to $100. Instead, you can use plastic, lidded containers, or you can make a bin from wood. I started out with a 33-gallon plastic box with a tight lid. However, I found that the box was too high with much wasted space. The top 10 inches were used by the worms only to deposit their eggs. I now use two 10-gallon plastic bins that yield twice the compost as the larger bin. The bins cost about $5 each. My worm-compost harvest has averaged 60 gallons a year.

Keep Worm Composting Going Through the Winter
—LYNETTE COURTNEY AND CAROL SCHMINKE

Cold worms seem to slow down and eat much less, inhibiting the composting process, so find a safe indoor location for your bin, protected from direct heat and cold, where temperatures stay between 50°F and 80°F.

Give Them Space, Moisture, and Air
—JOAN D. FILSINGER

Your worms will need roughly 1 square foot of surface area to digest each pound of waste material generated per week. You can always increase your composting operation, especially since your worms will reproduce when they are well fed.

A little moisture helps worms to wriggle. Add just enough water to a bedding mixture (such as peat moss) to make it as wet as a wrung-out sponge.

Cut up scraps to hasten composting. While worms will eat food scraps of any size, chopping them by hand or in a food processor cuts down on digestion time.

A little moisture helps worms to wriggle. Add just enough water to a bedding mixture (such as peat moss) to make it as wet as a wrung-out sponge. If the bedding becomes dry, spray or sprinkle water to spread the moisture evenly.

A worm bin needs to have drainage holes on the bottom and air holes above the level of the bedding. The holes should be ⅛ to ¼ inch wide. For a 10-gallon bin, I made eight drainage holes on the bottom and a total of 18 air holes in the lid and on the sides near the top. I first tried using a heated awl, but the holes were not big enough. So I plugged in my soldering iron and made holes just the right size. You can also make holes in soft plastic with a drill, a heated ice pick, or a knitting needle. If you are melting plastic, make sure you're in a well-ventilated area.

. . . .

Biodegradable Bedding Keeps Things Moist

—JOAN D. FILSINGER

To create the right environment, line your bin with biodegradable bedding. You can use peat moss, aged manure, sawdust, dried grass clippings, hay, garden loam, or even shredded cardboard, newspaper, grocery bags, and most types of shredded leaves. Oak and other highly acidic leaves are not recommended, since these worms don't like an acidic environment. It's not a good idea to use heavily colored or glossy paper, since they may have inks or other substances that are toxic to red worms.

Bury food scraps in the bedding, and let the worms come wriggling.

. . . .

Feed Your Worms a Well-Balanced Diet

—JOAN D. FILSINGER

With 2 pounds of worms, try starting out with about 1 cup of food scraps every other day. Observe how quickly they eat it up, and adjust your feeding routine accordingly. But don't worry—they can survive for weeks at a time without any fresh scraps.

Cut up scraps to hasten composting. Chopping them by hand or in a food processor cuts down on digestion time.

Aim for a variety of fruit and vegetable scraps, as well as leftover bread, pasta, and grains. While worms are able to digest animal and dairy products, these substances may cause disagreeable odors and attract flies. Avoid feeding them oils and fatty foods like peanut butter, which could become rancid.

Place the scraps on top of the bedding, or make a shallow hole in which to bury them. When burying, it helps to mark the spot with an object like a pencil and add the next feeding in another part of the bin.

Move the Bedding (and Turn On the Light) to Harvest the Compost

—JOAN D. FILSINGER

The easiest way to harvest the finished compost is simply to push the bedding and worms to one end of the box and fill the other end with fresh bedding and table scraps. Within a few weeks, the worms will munch their way over to the fresh food and you can scoop out the compost from the now deserted side of the bin.

Another way to harvest is to arrange a table covered with plastic under a 100-watt bulb so that the light is within 2 feet of the table. Heap the compost on the plastic in a cone-shaped mound. Any worms exposed to light will scurry to the center of the mound, letting you scoop away compost from the perimeter. Wait another 10 to 20 minutes and you can remove another layer of compost. Eventually, all the worms will have burrowed into a compact mass in the center of the pile. You can then move the worms back into the bin after lining it with new bedding.

Worms turn away from light. To make harvesting easier, use a light source to send worms scurrying inside a mound as compost is scraped off in layers.

2. Add water and air. A good compost pile has enough moisture to keep the microbes alive while still allowing air to penetrate the pile. It takes a good six to nine months to compost manure, depending on whether you are managing the pile actively (turning the pile periodically) or passively.

3. Use it wisely. Remember to use soil amendments responsibly and have your soil tested annually to be sure you are not applying more nutrients than your plants need. Excess nutrients, whether in the form of synthetic fertilizer or composted manure, can run off or leach into the environment and contaminate streams, lakes, and wells.

....

OTHER FERTILIZERS

Synthetic Fertilizers Should Be Strictly Supplemental
—DARYL BEYERS

They're manufactured products that bind plant nutrients into salt compounds that readily dissolve in water. Like table salt that dissolves in your pasta water, soluble fertilizers dissolve in the water in your watering can. In granular form spread upon the soil, slow-release fertilizers are dissolved by rain or irrigation. When synthetic fertilizers release their nutrients into the soil, they leave behind salts, which build up over time. Excessive salt can damage soil structure and dehydrate plants by drawing water from roots in the same way that salty foods dry out your lips.

....

A Synthetic Alternative to Bonemeal
—DICK BIR

Other sources of organic phosphorus include rock phosphates and colloidal phosphates. Both are relatively expensive and can be difficult to find. If you can find rock phosphates that list on the packaging a guaranteed analysis of the nutrient content, then using these according to directions is fine. I do not recommend using colloidal phosphates because their fine particles make them difficult to apply.

Cheaper synthetic alternatives offer high levels of phosphorus that are more immediately available to plants. However, super phosphates (0–20–0) and treble super phosphates (0–46–0) are made by treating minerals with acid and aren't considered natural or organic. Bulb

GET THE SCOOP ON SYNTHETIC FERTILIZER INGREDIENTS

Ingredient labels for organic fertilizers make sense: We're all well acquainted with manure, and if we use our imaginations, we can figure out where bonemeal comes from. But the labels on synthetic fertilizers are a different story. What are potassium phosphate and urea, and what do they do for our plants? Most gardeners know that the "12–4–8" represents the percentage of nitrogen, phosphorus, and potassium, respectively, but you are probably less familiar with these chemicals:

Urea supplies nitrogen. When given to plants, urea breaks down into ammonium. This chemical takes less energy for a plant to use than nitrate, the other nitrogen source for plants. But too much ammonium is toxic. Conveniently, ammonium in fertilizer converts naturally into nitrate over the course of days or weeks. Cold weather, however, slows down this conversion. When temperatures dip below 70°F, opt for fertilizers that contain more nitrate (such as potassium nitrate) and less urea or ammonium.

Potassium chloride consists of potassium and chlorine, both of which are quickly available to plants after the fertilizer is applied. Potassium is vital for growth and photosynthesis, while the chlorine simply makes the potassium water-soluble and easier for plants to absorb.

Potassium phosphate provides plants with phosphorus and more potassium. Plants need phosphorus to produce roots, fruit, and flowers. But too often, fertilizers contain more phosphorus than plants can use, and the excess runs off into waterways.

Disodium zinc EDTA, manganese EDTA, disodium salt, and **ferric sodium EDTA** are known as chelates, which are chemicals that provide nutrients over a wider range of pH values than would otherwise be possible. So while iron (in ferric sodium), manganese, and zinc are not normally available to plants in alkaline soils, they are when combined with EDTA as a chelate.

—JEFF GILLMAN

Booster®, a complete fertilizer (9–9–6) with some controlled-release forms of essential nutrients, is another alternative. This may be the most economical way to go when fertilizing bulbs because you would only need to apply one fertilizer once a year.

Serve Up the Right Amount of Nitrogen to Your Plants
—LEE REICH

Nitrogen is the most crucial and the most abundant, yet the most fleeting, of plant nutrients. It is the key component of plant chlorophyll, which, coupled with sunlight, fuels plant growth. Slow growth is often a symptom of a plant hungry for nitrogen. The presence of pale green or yellow leaves is another symptom of peckish plants. Conversely, too large a helping of nitrogen can make plants overly succulent and barely able to support themselves, resulting in split or broken stems. Springtime appetizers of organic fertilizers will serve up nitrogen right when your plants need it most.

Myth: If a Little Is Good, Twice as Much Is Better
—JOHN C. FECH

A precise measurement of fertilizers and pesticides is crucial to the health of your garden. If you like to watch the Food Network, you've probably seen Emeril Lagasse "kick it up a notch" by adding a little more of a certain spice. This approach may be fine for cooking, but it's not for gardening. Fertilizers can raise salt levels in the soil to toxic levels, burning the roots and stunting growth of your plants. Pesticides, when overused, can also have similar detrimental effects on plants by burning the leaves or raising toxicity levels in the soil. Garden products, both organic and synthetic, are extensively tested during research and development to provide safe and reliable results, so using the exact recommended dosage is the best practice.

Rhododendrons and Azaleas Have Different Nitrogen Needs
—LEE REICH

Plants that thrive in acidic soils, such as rhododendrons and azaleas (*Rhododendron* spp. and cvs.), naturally prefer their nitrogen served as ammonium. Therefore, if you choose to feed acid-loving plants with synthetic fertilizers, use a brand that contains ammonium sulfate. All organic fertilizers applied to acidic soils naturally end up as ammonium because the bacteria that convert ammonium to nitrate don't live in acidic soils.

Don't Count on Foliar Feeding to Keep Your Plants Healthy
—LINDA CHALKER SCOTT

Although traditional fertilizers are sometimes affected by leaching, chemical reactions, and microbial activity, which can all decrease what actually reaches the plant, they are still a better option than foliar fertilizers. Fertilizers applied to the leaf do not travel throughout the rest of the plant. They just stay right in the leaf, but the nutrients are often also needed in other tissues.

Fish-Based Fertilizers Can Be Valuable Natural Sources of Nutrients

—MARK GASKELL

Fish emulsions and other liquid and dried fish materials, manufactured as by-products from fish processing, are easy to apply. All of these fish-derived fertilizers, however, are primarily organic forms of nutrients and will need to undergo further bacterial decomposition for the nutrients to be available for plant uptake. If the fertilizer is needed to quickly correct a deficiency, a more soluble form of conventional fertilizer may be a better choice.

All fish fertilizers (dried fish powder, liquid fish material, and fish emulsion) smell while in the container. I do not believe that the smell will attract wild animals, but it may attract flies if the product is stored in bulk. The smell, however, usually dissipates once the fertilizer is diluted into an irrigation system or added to the soil.

Hold Off on Biochar . . . for Now

—LINDA CHALKER-SCOTT

Biochar is baked organic material. It's the charcoal left over from pyrolysis, a process in biofuel production that involves slowly cooking organic matter at high temperatures without oxygen. A finished biochar depends on its feedstock: A switchgrass biochar, for instance, is different from one made of yard waste or wooden pallets. And variable temperatures and rates of cooking also produce different characteristics.

From improving drainage to boosting soil fertility, biochar has an impressive list of advantages. But it's still too soon to recommend biochars for home gardens because most of the research has focused on crop production. We still don't know how biochars affect home gardens. But we do know that adding too much or the wrong kind of biochar can harm earthworms, bind nutrients too tightly, make soil too alkaline or saline, saturate clay soils, and reduce pesticide effectiveness. So for now, it's best to let the science catch up with our enthusiasm for this new product.

Before You Feed a Plant Under Stress, Find the Cause

—JOHN C. FECH

Fertilizer is added to plants growing in poor soils and to plants that show symptoms of lacking a particular nutrient. Generally, when a plant is stressed, it's not from lack of food. Compacted soil, heat, salt spray, faulty planting, and improper placement are usually the culprits that stress plants. It is important to rule out other environmental conditions before deciding a plant is under-fertilized. When fed, stressed plants use up energy that is better spent on growing roots, warding off decay organisms, or defending against insects.

WATER

WATERING WELL

Avoid Certain Plants If You Have Hard Water

—GEORGE ELLIOT

Water hardness and softness can have a significant effect on plants. Hardness is related to the content of calcium carbonate and magnesium carbonate dissolved in the water, often expressed in units of grains per gallon. You may recognize that calcium carbonate and magnesium carbonate are the components of limestone. When hard water is used for irrigation, it's the same as adding a small amount of lime every time you water. Over time, this continual addition of lime will increase the pH of the growing medium. Rainfall helps to counteract it; nevertheless, hard water can still cause some problems when irrigating.

Some plants—most notably petunias and acid-loving plants like azaleas—are sensitive to high pH levels. An increase in pH causes young leaves to turn pale and yellowish, while leaf veins remain green, sometimes referred to as a lime-induced chlorosis. It won't kill the plant, but it will make it look unhealthy and reduce its vigor.

Will Sunshine Focused Through Water Droplets Burn Leaves?

—JOHN C. FECH

The diffused rays of the sun are not powerful enough to cause burning. If it were the case that water droplets burned leaves, farmers would encounter huge losses after each daytime rainstorm. In fact, lawn-care professionals often cool turf by spritzing water over the foliage during the hottest part of the day. In general, the best time to water most garden plants is early in the morning, because of higher municipal water pressure, a lower evaporation rate, and the potential to reduce foliar diseases that often occur in overly moist situations. But if you are left with no other choice, watering midday will not harm your plants.

Don't Use Softened Water for Irrigation

—GEORGE ELLIOT

If you have hard water, you should not use softened water for irrigation. Softened water has a high salt (sodium chloride) content, which causes its own set of problems. Regrettably, there is no practical way to counteract hard water. The best solution is to refrain from using overhead irrigation, regularly check and maintain drip-irrigation systems, and avoid plants that are susceptible to lime-induced chlorosis.

5. Overtightening hose connections or nozzles crushes the washer and can even cut through it. A little bit tighter than snug is just right.

6. Inspect washers regularly, and replace them at least once a year.

7. If you have plastic hose ends, take care not to cross-thread when attaching the hose to a bib or to nozzles made of metal.

8. Be careful not to step on or drive over hose ends. Once they have lost their shape, they will not properly seal and must be replaced.

9. Even solid-brass fittings will leak if you continually drop a hose or drag it across pavement.

10. Keep your hose away from oils and solvents, which will degrade the material.

Be Careful When Using Rooftop-Harvested Water on Edibles
—REBECCA CHESIN

Most experts advise against using rooftop-harvested rainwater for edible plants. There have been few safety studies, but roofs contain all sorts of materials that rain will wash off into your barrels: chemicals leached from your roofing materials, dust, plant matter blown by the wind, bird droppings, and bacteria.

Get a Bigger Bang per Bucket
—JOHN BRAY

Consider the life cycle of the plants in your garden when you water. Recent transplants, for example, need frequent light watering to accommodate their shallow young roots and ease the shock of being pulled from their six-packs. For some crops, like tomatoes, yields may improve but some flavor may be lost with too much watering as fruit ripens. And with carrots and cabbages, watering should be reduced as the crop reaches maturity to keep the vegetables from splitting. Once plants are established, more harm than good is done by giving them a daily sprinkling. If only the soil surface gets wet, roots will look up, not down, for their drinks. Deep, less frequent watering works best.

A Cheap and Easy Way to Water a New Tree or Shrub

Drill a 1⁄16-inch-diameter hole near the bottom of a 5-gallon plastic bucket and dab paint over the hole so that you can see it with a quick glance. Fill the bucket with water, and place it with the hole facing the root zone of the tree or shrub, where it can deliver a slow, steady stream of water. You can easily mix water-soluble fertilizer in the water, thereby getting two jobs done at the same time.

PROS AND CONS OF FAVORITE WATERING METHODS

METHOD	ADVANTAGE	DISADVANTAGE
Direct-to-Soil Delivery with Soaker Hoses	Less water is lost to wind evaporation, and water reaches odd corners not covered by overhead sprinklers.	Soaker hoses are often covered with mulch for aesthetic reasons and become vulnerable to sharp garden tools. No cleansing water hits foliage to rinse dust away and keep mite populations down.
Overhead Delivery by Manually Placed Sprinkler System on Timing Device	Water is applied when needed. Where summers are hot but it does rain, this method may be necessary only four or five times a season.	Hose wrestling is required, and water is not directed to roots.
Point Irrigation Direct to Soil with Watering Can or Wand Hose Attachment	Water is applied only where and when needed. Water can be directed to plants that need it most.	This method can be time-consuming. Hose wrestling is required. Watering system breaks down in gardener's absence.
Point Irrigation Trickled by Emitter	No water is wasted in weed zones between plants, and little is lost to wind and evaporation.	Gardener must check soil moisture levels near emitters, or overwatering can occur. Emitters may clog and plants may dry out. Expanding root systems require repositioning of emitters.
Overhead Delivery by In-Ground Sprinkler System on Timing Device	No hose wrestling required, and water keeps flowing even when the gardener is absent.	Gardener falls out of the watering loop and fails to notice a watering problem until it becomes a crisis situation.

—JANET MACUNOVICH

TOP 25 NATIVE PLANTS BY REGION

Northeast

SUMMERSWEET
(*Clethra alnifolia* and cvs.) offers delicious-smelling flowers and good fall color.
USDA hardiness zones: 3 to 9
Size: 6 to 8 feet tall and wide
Conditions: Full sun to partial shade; moist, fertile, acidic, well-drained soil

Summersweet is a wonderful shrub that offers 3- to 5-inch-long spiky white flowers that possess a strong, spicy fragrance in late summer. The dark green foliage turns pale to golden yellow in fall, and old seed heads will persist through winter, giving this plant some off-season appeal. Summersweet is an adaptable species, growing in moist, shady woodland conditions as well as hot, dry, sunny exposures in sandy soils. This shrub generally works well in mixed borders and is a great companion for most herbaceous plants. It will also attract a wide variety of pollinators to the garden. If you simply don't have the space for the straight species, try 'Compacta', which features a dense habit that's only 5 to 6 feet tall and wide but has the same magnificently fragrant flowers as well as unusually dark green foliage.

Summersweet (*Clethra alnifolia*)

WINTERBERRY
(*Ilex verticillata*) is a wonderful deciduous holly that typically grows near streams and ponds.
Zones: 5 to 8
Size: 6 to 10 feet tall and wide
Conditions: Full sun to partial shade; moist, well-drained soil

It provides a great show in fall and early winter, with golden yellow foliage and clusters of glossy, bright red fruit on each stem. But remember that fruiting hollies generally need a male pollinator close by. The berries of winterberry are prized by many bird species, including the northern cardinals and American robins.

Winterberry (*Ilex verticillata*)

LITTLE BLUESTEM
(*Schizachyrium scoparium* and cvs.) is one of the most spectacular native grasses out there.
Zones: 2 to 7
Size: 2 to 3 feet tall and wide
Conditions: Full sun; fertile, well-drained soil

With its blue-green foliage in spring and summer that turns brilliant shades of golden yellow to reddish bronze in fall and winter, this grass never disappoints. Soft, silvery white seed heads form later in the season and will persist even when the plant is dormant. Masses of little bluestem will illuminate the winter landscape. Although typically seen along roadsides and in wild, natural areas, little bluestem is now being used in cultivated gardens as well. There are, in fact, several cultivars with even deeper blue summer foliage that offer great appeal.

Flowering dogwood (*Cornus florida* and cvs.)

Little bluestem (*Schizachyrium scoparium* and cvs.)

FLOWERING DOGWOOD

(*Cornus florida* and cvs.) is a great East Coast species that has seen a renaissance over the past decade.

Zones: 5 to 8

Size: 20 to 30 feet tall and wide

Conditions: Full sun to partial shade; rich, moist, well-drained soil

There is nothing quite like the striking white and pink bracts that surround the tree's yellowish green flowers in spring. After the flowers finish putting on their show, rich, dark green summer foliage emerges, changing to brilliant shades of orange, crimson, and purple by fall. The clusters of red fruit usually don't last long because birds eat them rather quickly. But flowering dogwood has winter interest, too: from its rounded, upright habit; rough alligator skin–like bark; and silver-gray buds that glisten in the winter sun.

—VINCENT A. SIMEONE

Mid-Atlantic

BUTTERFLY WEED

(*Asclepias tuberosa*) thrives under less-than-ideal conditions.

Zones: 4 to 9

Size: Up to 3 feet tall and 2 to 3 feet wide

Conditions: Full sun; sandy or gravelly, well-drained soil

This herbaceous perennial's bright orange blossoms provide nectar for at least six species of butterflies and countless beneficial insects and pollinators. Its leaves also provide larval food for monarch caterpillars. Butterfly weed is a taprooted plant that is found naturally in dry fields and shale barrens. In fall, silken seeds burst from mature pods and waft toward new sites to create oases for pollinators and migrating monarch butterflies. Although the plant is in the milkweed family, it lacks the trademark white sap, and it does not spread aggressively, like common milkweed. Now at risk of extinction in five Northeast states, this plant is a must-have for any dry, sunny landscape.

Butterfly weed (*Asclepias tuberosa*)

SASSAFRAS

(*Sassafras albidum*) plants exude a spicy, pleasant aroma.

Zones: 4 to 8

Size: Up to 60 feet tall and wide

Conditions: Full sun to partial shade; moist, acidic, well-drained soil

Sassafras delights year-round: In spring, its unpretentious chartreuse flowers are followed by leaves unfurling into three distinct shapes: three lobed, mitten shaped, and simple (no lobes). In late summer, birds love to visit the dark blue drupes (or berries), cupped atop bright red stalks. In fall, the leaves turn shades of orange, red, and yellow. And in winter, its deeply fissured bark and crooked stems add texture to a barren landscape. The leaves provide larval food for the promethean silk moth and spicebush swallowtail butterfly.

Sassafras (*Sassafras albidum*)

PAWPAW

(*Asimina triloba*) is the largest edible fruit native to North America and is rich in amino acids.

Zones: 6 to 8

Size: Up to 20 feet tall and wide

Conditions: Full sun to partial shade; moist, fertile, slightly acidic, well-drained soil

The pawpaw tree provides visual interest galore, with droopy, tropical-like leaves; small maroon flowers; and lumpy fruit that ripens on the branches. Zebra swallowtail caterpillars feed exclusively on its leaves, and the fruit is eaten by box turtles and small mammals. A prehistoric tree that is older than bees, pawpaw is pollinated by beetles and flies. It fruits best in full sun, and its flowers must be cross-pollinated from genetically distinct plants and pollinated by hand if beetles or flies are not present.

—SUSAN TANTSITS AND LOUISE SCHAEFER

Pawpaw (*Asimina triloba*)

Midwest

TWINLEAF

(*Jeffersonia diphylla*) is an exciting woodland gem—from start to finish.

Zones: 5 to 7

Size: 12 to 18 inches tall and 1 foot wide

Conditions: Dappled to full shade; moist, rich, slightly acidic to slightly neutral, well-drained soil

Perhaps my favorite woodland wildflower, this underutilized native is fun to watch from spring to autumn. Twinleaf emerges before the trees leaf out, its purplish foliage and stems exploding out of the ground, turning green with hints of copper, then producing their individually borne, 1-inch-wide glistening white flowers—all in a matter of days. Watch closely for the blossoms because they are, at best, fleeting. Twinleaf will remain in foliage well into summer and maybe even autumn. The 6-inch-long, blue-green summer leaves are so deeply divided that each leaf looks like the pair of wings of a luna moth. Older plants form handsome mounds of foliage. You will be rewarded the following spring with self-sown seedlings that you can share with friends.

Twinleaf (*Jeffersonia diphylla*)

BOTTLE GENTIAN

(*Gentiana andrewsii*) is a harbinger of autumn, with its month-long late-summer to early-fall display of 1950s-era rocket ship–shaped flowers in various shades of rich blue to violet.
Zones: 3 to 7
Size: 1 to 2 feet tall and 12 to 18 inches wide
Conditions: Full sun to dappled shade; moist, rich, acidic to neutral soil

Bottle gentian
(*Gentiana andrewsii*)

Pry one of the flower tips open and take a close look at its wonderfully fringed and striped pleats. Be on the lookout for the bumblebees lurking inside! Plant by the oodles in moist shade gardens, prairies, or wildflower meadows. Plants will clump up nicely over time.

ROYAL CATCHFLY

(*Silene regia*), with its clusters of scarlet flowers, is guaranteed to incite hummingbird turf battles for the duration of its July and August bloom.
Zones: 4 to 8
Size: 2 to 4 feet tall and 1 to 2 feet wide
Conditions: Full sun to light shade; rocky or sandy, well-drained soil

Royal catchfly is a rare species in the wild, but fortunately it is amenable to cultivation in well-drained soil. The stems are spindly, so cultivate it with the support of surrounding plants—but not to the point of shading it. If you touch its sticky stems, leaves, and green calyx tubes, you'll understand how the plant got its common name.

Royal catchfly (*Silene regia*)

PLAINS FALSE INDIGO

(*Baptisia leucophaea*, syn. *B. bracteata* var. *leucophaea*) is the earliest of the false indigos to bloom, and it is admired for its copious, oversize cream to butter yellow flowers.
Zones: 3 to 8
Size: 1 to 2 feet tall and 18 to 48 inches wide
Conditions: Full sun to light shade; moist to dry, well-drained soil

Plains false indigo won't swallow its neighbors as will its more robust relative, the blue false indigo (*B. australis*, Zones 3–9). Plant plains false indigo at the edge of a border, in prairie restorations, and in meadow openings where the flowers can readily be seen. Stems can go dormant by late summer, so plant individually rather than en masse so that the holes created by its dormancy aren't conspicuous.

Plains false indigo (*Baptisia leucophaea*)

MICHIGAN LILY

(*Lillium michiganense*) has early-summer turkscap flowers in gaudy shades of yellow, orange, and red with purple-brown spotting and will be visited by a plethora of hummingbirds, moths, and butterflies seeking its nectar.

Zones: 3 to 7

Size: 2 to 5 feet tall and 1 foot wide

Conditions: Full sun to dappled shade; moist, rich, well-drained soil

Michigan lily is native in areas from wet meadows and prairies to low woodlands and swamp edges. Under favorable conditions, the rhizomatous bulbs will form modest clumps. As with many lilies, this one prefers its feet in the shade and its head in the sun. Plant in fall only, and mulch the bulbs. Be sure to protect it from deer and rabbits, which delight in mowing it down.

—JIM AULT

Michigan lily (*Lillium michiganense*)

Southern Plains

VIOLET TWINING SNAPDRAGON
(*Maurandella antirrhiniflora*) is a delicate yet vigorous twiner that sports luminous green triangular leaves and offers violet to rosy pink blooms throughout the warm months of the year.

Zones: 9 to 11

Size: Vining 6 to 10 feet

Conditions: Full sun to light shade; moist, well-drained soil

Looking for a dainty climber that won't overwhelm that cute little trellis you just found at a garage sale? Violet twining snapdragon is fitting for a small frame, rambling unceremoniously over an old woodpile or hanging casually from a bluff. It's not a true snapdragon but a relative. It is favored as a host plant for the common buckeye butterfly, but thankfully, it's generally not relished by deer.

Violet twining snapdragon (*Maurandella antirrhiniflora*)

HOP TREE

(*Ptelea trifoliata*) is a fragrant delight.

Zones: 5 to 9

Size: 15 feet tall and 10 feet wide

Conditions: Full sun to partial shade; moist to dry, well-drained soil

Despite what its two common names—wafer ash and hop tree—might lead you to believe, this plant is neither an ash nor a hop but rather a member of the citrus family. Hop tree, however, is a mainstay for the orange dog, the citrus-orchard pest name for the ravenous caterpillar of the otherwise beloved giant swallowtail butterfly. Feeding the anticipation and delight of humans and small pollinators alike, a scrumptious vanilla-clove aroma perfumes the air come spring, when this understory tree unfolds its clusters of tiny yellowish green flowers. Its true elegance lies in the ascending, interwoven light gray branches, which look their best under the skilled hands of a master pruner. At its mature height, hop tree won't interfere with power lines. And its bitter, papery fruit, called a samara, has been used as a substitute for hops in brewing beer. What more could you ask of just one plant?

Prairie rain lily (*Zephyranthes drummondii*)

Hop tree (*Ptelea trifoliata*)

PRAIRIE RAIN LILY

(*Zephyranthes drummondii*, syn. *Cooperia pedunculata*) surprises with beautiful blooms for a spring treat.

Zones: 7 to 10

Size: 1 foot tall and wide

Conditions: Full sun to partial shade; well-drained soil

Like an ethereal angel, the ephemeral prairie rain lily epitomizes purity. Its strappy, gray-green leaves can easily hide in lawns when planted en masse or among other low-growing plants. Then, as perhaps a forgotten surprise, the flowers burst out of seemingly nowhere for a few short days after a good rain in spring and early summer. Lightly fragrant upon emerging, the 2-inch-wide trumpets top single, unbranched stems. They open at dusk and fade to translucent pink the following morning.

TEXAS SACAHUISTA

(*Nolina texana*) adds rich texture to any garden.

Zones: 5 to 9

Size: 3 feet tall and 4 to 6 feet wide

Conditions: Full sun to partial shade; well-drained soil

With virtually no maintenance, this woody lily (yes, technically it's a lily) makes an audacious statement in grand swaths, as a solitary focal point, or as an accent in

Texas sacahuista (*Nolina texana*)

a large container. Its long slender leaves flow from a woody base with firm gracefulness. With a fluid arching form, Texas sacahuista evokes flowing water and looks great pouring over rocks, over a wall, or down a hillside. Clusters of tiny cream-colored flowers barely emerge above the wave of leaves in mid- to late spring. This deer-resistant, leathery evergreen is best adapted to dry, shaded woodlands but takes full sun if treated to extra moisture.

Mountain West

'COOMBE'S WINTER GLOW' BEAVERTAIL CACTUS

(*Opuntia aurea* 'Coombe's Winter Glow') has pads that are a rich burgundy-purple in winter.

Zones: 5 to 10

Size: 10 inches tall and up to 5 feet wide

Conditions: Full sun; dry, well-drained soil

Can anything be easier to grow than this great cactus? Drop it on the ground and your work is done! (And while that may be true, I recommend actually planting it.) The pads root easily, thrive in full hot sun, and are unfazed by drought. By spring, the pads return to blue-green, with fat buds that burst into crepe-papery, hot pink blooms for several weeks. 'Coombe's Winter Glow' beavertail cactus lacks long spines but still has tiny glochids that are irritating, so handle with care. Any dry border will be enhanced by this cactus.

'Coombe's Winter Glow'
(*Opuntia aurea* 'Coombe's Winter Glow')

BABY BLUE RABBITBRUSH

(*Chrysothamnus nauseosus* var. *nauseosus*, syn. *Ericameria nauseosus* var. *nauseosus*) gilds the roadsides of the West in gold each September and October, providing a late-summer feast for native pollinators.

Zones: 4 to 9

Size: 2 feet tall and 3 feet wide

Conditions: Full sun to partial shade; well-drained soil

Baby blue rabbitbrush is a compact and hardy Colorado variety that forms a perfect blue-green dome all summer, transforming to gold as the days shorten. Fluffy seed heads add interest all winter, and an easy spring trim to 6 to 8 inches tall will ensure a uniform habit.

Baby blue rabbitbrush (*Chrysothamnus nauseosus*)

BRISTLECONE PINE

(*Pinus aristata*) is the quintessential symbol of the rugged high country in the West.

Zones: 4 to 7

Size: Up to 20 feet tall and 15 feet wide

Conditions: Full sun; well-drained soil, drought tolerant when established

Despite its high-elevation origins, it is quite adaptable to life down among the rest of us. In habitat, the tree is windswept and gnarled with age and can live for more than 2,000 years. In the garden, expect the densely bristled branches to add about 6 inches a year, with the tree forming a pyramidal shape in its youth. After many years, bristlecone pine takes on a more irregular character. These qualities can be enhanced by judicious pruning throughout its life, creating a sculpted specimen to pass on to the next generation.

Bristlecone pine (*Pinus aristata*)

Golden columbine (*Aquilegia chrysantha*)

Southern California

LANCELEAF LIVEFOREVER
(*Dudleya lanceolata*) gets its name from its linear olive-colored leaves.

Zones: 9 to 10

Size: 6 inches tall and 1 foot wide

Conditions: Full sun to partial shade; well-drained soil

In Southern California, you'll find lanceleaf liveforever growing in the peninsular mountain ranges east of Los Angeles and San Diego. It sends up flower stalks that attract hummingbirds and other pollinators, and it is recognized as an outstanding performer in containers and rock gardens. When planting, position lanceleaf liveforever at a 30-degree angle. This will ensure the sharp drainage the species prefers. Artfully grouped amid rocks or with a piece of deadwood, this succulent can easily create a striking native bonsai.

GOLDEN COLUMBINE

(*Aquilegia chrysantha* and cvs.) seems almost magical when found in the wild.

Zones: 3 to 8

Size: 30 inches tall and 15 inches wide

Conditions: Full sun to full shade; average, well-drained soil

Golden columbine's delicate tufts of leaves perched on shaded red sandstone ledges or flanking hidden springs are a welcome delight in the arid Southwest. Despite this sense of rarity, this is one of the easiest and most persistent columbines for the garden. Most soils suit it, and it will reseed itself readily in thin gravel mulch. The bloom season lasts from spring until frost, improved by deadheading. Thriving in full sun, it is also especially welcome in dryish shade. If other varieties are growing nearby, hybrids in various color combinations will result.

—DAN JOHNSON

Lanceleaf liveforever (*Dudleya lanceolata*)

'HOWARD MCMINN' MANZANITA

(*Arctostaphylos densiflora* 'Howard McMinn') is stunning—from its blooms to its bark.

Zones: 7 to 9

Size: 6 to 10 feet tall and wide

Conditions: Full sun to partial shade; well-drained soil

With its chocolaty red bark, architectural branching pattern, and winter display of flower clusters, this plant exemplifies the beauty of California's chaparral. It remains a mystery to me why this shrub isn't more popular. 'Howard McMinn' manzanita puts to rest all myths regarding the finicky nature of this genus. It adapts well to many soil types and microclimates and to pruning; it even tolerates occasional summer irrigation under the proper conditions. This manzanita also boasts wildlife value as a nectar source for the monarch butterfly. It is known for attracting hummingbirds, too, which is sure to make it a focal point for any Southern California garden.

'Winifred Gilman' Cleveland sage
(*Salvia clevelandii* 'Winifred Gilman')

'WINIFRED GILMAN' CLEVELAND SAGE

(*Salvia clevelandii* 'Winifred Gilman') is a favorite due to its incredibly aromatic nature— it smells like a mixture of sunblock and chaparral.

Zones: 8 to 10

Size: 4 feet tall and wide

Conditions: Full sun; well-drained soil

'Winifred Gilman' Cleveland sage is native to the dry slopes of San Diego County's coastal plant community. Its benefits include a late bloom (it is one of the last to flower in my garden) and a compact, upright habit. Use it in containers, in rock gardens, on slopes, or in a transitional area, such as a perennial bed. It is adaptable to many soil conditions and microclimates and is a hummingbird magnet.

'Howard McMinn' Manzanita
(*Arctostaphylos densiflora* 'Howard McMinn')

SEASIDE DAISY

Erigeron glaucus is a favorite front-of-the-border plant for the garden.

Zones: 5 to 8

Size: 1 foot tall and 2 feet wide

Conditions: Full sun (along the coast) to partial shade (inland); well-drained soil

Seaside daisy—as its name implies—belongs to the daisy family and is commonly found along the central and northern coast of California, especially in the Monterey area. With regular deadheading and moderate supplemental irrigation during summer, seaside daisy will bloom nearly year-round. Its low-growing, cheerful flower groupings attract hummingbirds, butterflies, and positive comments from passersby. If used inland, place this species carefully, as its foliage will parch if not protected from the afternoon sun.

TOYON

(*Heteromeles arbutifolia*) is recognized as a hardy plant, adaptable to most soil types and microclimates—from the shade of mixed forest and oak woodland to the full sun of coastal sage scrub and chaparral.

Zones: 7 to 10

Size: 12 feet tall and wide

Conditions: Full sun to full shade; dry to poor, well-drained soil

California's European settlers, thinking the leaves and berries of this plant resembled English holly, called it Christmas berry. This, coupled with its abundance in the area of what is now Hollywood, is believed to be the reason for the city's namesake. Toyon's signature red berries appear in winter but begin in spring as white flower clusters that have a spicy aroma, attracting butterflies and a wide variety of birds.

— ROB MOORE

Seaside daisy (*Erigeron glaucus*)

Toyon (*Heteromeles arbutifolia*)

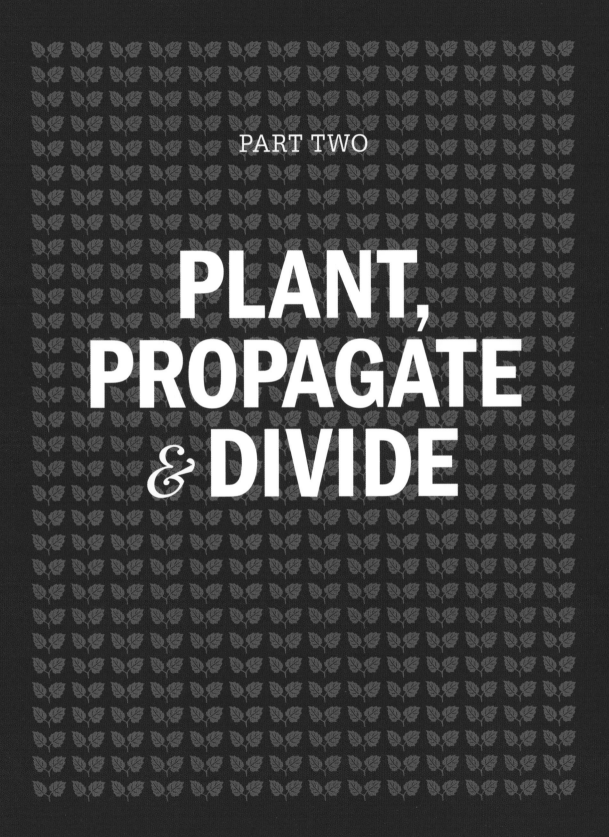

PART TWO

PLANT, PROPAGATE & DIVIDE

PLANT

BUY THE BEST PLANTS

Don't Always Choose the Plant With the Open Flowers
—JASON AND SHELLEY POWELL

Gardeners shopping at the nursery get the most excited about plants covered in flowers. But there's no rule that says you have to buy them. Unless you are unfamiliar with the plant's flower color and concerned about how it will look in your garden, we suggest you buy fall-blooming plants in spring and spring bloomers in fall. Your plants will have more time to get established in your garden, focusing on growth instead of flowers. If you must buy a plant during its season of bloom, select one with flower buds rather than open flowers. And if you have an annual, and it has plenty of buds but is a little leggy, look for new growth closer to the soil. These young leaves reveal the plant's vigor, and you can cut the leggy stems back to the young foliage and let that take over.

Look for Healthy Growth Aboveground
—JASON AND SHELLEY POWELL

Examine the leaves and stems of your plant. Check for any unusual spots, discolored leaves, or signs of insects. The time of year affects a plant's appearance; many plants look bedraggled by late summer. If you doubt a plant's health, ask the nursery person. As you assess the plants before you, keep two things in mind: A little discoloration doesn't mean you have a bad plant, and new growth generally indicates good health.

Next, look at the shape of the plant. The more stems a plant has, the better. Numerous stems indicate that the plant is more mature than a plant with few stems and that it will immediately provide you with increased growth. If the plant keeps its foliage low to the ground instead of holding it on tall stems, choose fuller growth over height or flowers. Also, look for several crowns (the points from which the foliage emerges), because it means you'll have more plants to start in your garden.

Look for Healthy, White Roots

—JASON AND SHELLEY POWELL

Gently turn over the container, and slide the plant out. Your nursery person won't mind this practice unless you don't return the plant to its container. Look for healthy, white roots and some soil. Don't buy the plant if you see roots that are brown and mushy or eaten by insects.

If the roots are so tight that you can't see the soil, then your plant is root-bound. You will need to loosen the roots with your hand or a knife prior to planting. It's acceptable to buy a root-bound plant, but it will mean increased stress for the plant and more effort for you. The larger the container holding the plant, the less tolerant you should be of a root-bound condition. Shrubs, especially ones that are 5 gallons or larger, seem to undergo more stress when transplanted after being root-bound.

PERENNIALS

Plant in Masses

— KERRY A. MENDEZ

More is better, right? Yes, if you are referring to time-saving design strategies for gardens and hard-to-plant areas in your landscape. When designing or reworking garden beds, make it easy on yourself by planting fewer varieties but in greater numbers. By doing so, you reduce the number of different maintenance tasks and tools required by applying the same repetitive motion longer to a greater number of plants (this also allows for safer daydreaming).

Many of us curse bugleweed (*Ajuga* spp. and cvs., Zones 3–9), sweet woodruff (*Galium odoratum*, Zones 5–8), creeping phlox (*Phlox subulata* cvs., Zones 3–8), and other ground covers, labeling them thugs. In all fairness, however, they are only doing what comes naturally to them: covering ground. Take advantage of those tough, free-spirited roots, and plant them in hell strips under shallow-rooted trees or on slopes where mowing is a challenge.

Five Fast-Growing Perennials That Flower Their First Year From Seed

—*FINE GARDENING* EDITORS

Blackberry lily
(*Iris Domestica*)

1. BLACKBERRY LILY (*IRIS DOMESTICA*)

In early summer, stems emerging from strappy foliage produce vivid orange, 2-inch flowers speckled with red. Seed heads split open in fall to reveal shiny black seeds.

Garden use: Great vertical accent for softer, mounded shapes. A good companion for blue flowers, or for hot-colored gardens of yellows, reds, and oranges.

Culture: Thrives in full sun and well-drained soil. Mulch in cold winter areas. Zones 5–10.

Seed-starting tips: Start indoors 10 to 12 weeks before last spring frost for earliest blooms. Seeds may take 3 weeks to sprout but then grow quickly.

2. BLANKET FLOWER (*GAILLARDIA* × *GRANDIFLORA*)

Bright, two-toned daisy flowers have red-brown centers and a vivid rim of yellow on the petals. The foliage is rough and hairy. Plants grow 2 to 3 feet tall by about 1½ feet wide.

Garden use: Reliable though often short-lived perennial for the middle of the garden. Combine with sunny yellow coreopsis, true-blue bachelor's buttons (*Centaurea cyanus*), or ornamental grasses.

Culture: Full sun. Almost any well-drained soil. Tolerates drought. Self-sows moderately. Zones 3–8.

Seed-starting tips: Very easy from seed. No special treatment needed. Start indoors 6 to 8 weeks before last spring frost.

Blanket flower
(*Gaillardia* × *grandiflora*)

Gaura (*Gaura lindheimeri*)

3. GAURA (*GAURA LINDHEIMERI*)

Gaura is a large, airy plant with delicate white flowers like a flock of butterflies on slender stems. It blooms from early summer to fall and grows 3 to 4 feet tall by 2 feet wide.

Garden use: Gaura's delicate, see-through quality makes it suitable for the middle or front of the garden. Beautiful with blue Russian sage (*Perovskia atriplicifolia*) and pinks (*Dianthus* spp.).

Culture: Full sun. Absolutely well-drained soil. Thrives in drought, heat, and humidity. Zones 6–9.

Seed-starting tips: Seed germinates in about 2 weeks. No special treatment needed. Sow indoors 8 to 10 weeks before last spring frost.

4. ROSE CAMPION (*LYCHNIS CORONARIA*)

Rose campion is a cottage-garden favorite with felted, silvery white foliage and stems accented in summer by cerise flowers atop the branching stems. The plant grows to 2½ feet tall and 1½ feet wide.

Garden use: Create a cottage-garden jumble with biennial dame's rocket (*Hesperis matronalis*), bachelor's buttons, hollyhocks (*Alcea* spp.), old roses, and other informal plants.

Culture: Full sun. Rich, well-drained soil. Short-lived, but self-sows to replace itself. Zones 4–8.

Seed-starting tips: Scarify seed before starting indoors 6 to 8 weeks before last spring frost.

Rose campion
(*Lychnis coronaria*)

Black-eyed Susan
(*Rudbeckia fulgida*)

5. BLACK-EYED SUSAN (*RUDBECKIA FULGIDA*)

This familiar, beloved daisy has golden petals and a dark, central disk. It blooms in summer and grows to 2½ feet tall and 2 feet across.

Garden use: Indispensable, thanks to its abundant, long-blooming flowers. Combines well with ornamental grasses, blazing star (*Liatris* spp.), and sunflowers (*Helianthus annuus* cvs.).

Culture: Full sun. Average, well-drained soil. Drought tolerant. Zones 4–9.

Seed-starting tips: Seed is simple to start. Sow indoors 6 to 8 weeks before last spring frost.

Buy the Wisteria That Will Bloom

—MEGHAN RAY

The most common reason for lack of flowers in wisteria is the selection of a seed-grown plant over a grafted plant. Grafted plants typically bloom within three years, while seed-grown vines may take upward of seven years before flowering—if ever.

Don't Buy Rampant Reseeders

—KERRY A. MENDEZ

When selecting plants, be cautious of rapid self-sowers. If a plant is known as a "fertile myrtle," leave it on the garden-center shelf. Plant tags, unfortunately, don't usually state if a plant is overly generous with its seeds; we usually find this out through trial and error or from exasperated fellow gardeners. So do your homework. Some reseeders to beware of include mallows (*Malva* spp. and cvs., Zones 3–8), bachelor's buttons (*Centaurea montana* and cvs., Zones 3–9), black-eyed Susans (*Rudbeckia* spp. and cvs., Zones 3–11), and most biennials. If you simply must have the plant, stay on top of deadheading; otherwise, the free-spirited progeny will germinate wherever the breeze may carry them.

Give Sedge the Edge

—ROY DIBLIK

Sedges have a grasslike appearance, but unlike most ornamental grasses, many perform as well or better in shade as they do in sun. For that reason, they can fill a useful design niche. Sedges are mostly grown for their bladelike foliage, which ranges from thin strands to thick straps in shades of green, bluish green, yellow, and copper. They're durable and make adaptable garden companions.

Sedges with bright, unusual, or variegated foliage make dramatic specimen or accent plants in borders or containers. And those with subtle foliage make elegant ground covers and can soften the edges of borders. They mix well with other perennials and help create a well-balanced planting.

Cutting-Garden Essentials

—CATHERINE MIX

If you only grow a handful of vase-worthy flowers, these are the ones you need.

Festiva Maxima peony (Zones 3–8; grows 2 to 3 feet tall and wide). This double-blossom cultivar is fairly easy to grow, preferring full sun and well-drained soil.

Giant white calla lily (Zones 8–10; can reach 3 feet tall and 2 feet wide). This plant thrives in full sun and rich, sandy soil. It needs to stay evenly moist, so a thick layer of mulch is a good idea.

'Pacific Giants Mix' delphinium (Zones 3–7; reaches 5 feet tall and 2 feet wide). With full sun and fertile, well-drained soil, this delphinium blooms from early summer to midsummer.

'Elfin Pink' penstemon (Zones 4–9; 1 foot tall and wide). A spiky flower that looks great in petite arrangements. When planted in full sun and fertile, well-drained soil, it will produce blooms from early summer to early fall.

Drumstick plants (Zones 9–11; 2 feet tall and 5 inches wide). Flower heads appear all summer; they like full sun and well-drained soil. They also dry beautifully.

'Dreaming Spires' Siberian iris (Zones 3–8; reaches 3 feet tall). Easy to grow, this iris prefers full sun and evenly moist soil. Blooms from mid-spring to early summer.

'Purpleicious' speedwell (Zones 4–8; 8 to 12 inches tall). Searing violet blooms are prolific and last a long time as cut flowers. Relatively low maintenance, it tolerates poor soil to some degree.

'Butterfly Blue' pincushion flower (Zones 3–8; 16 inches tall and wide). It has lovely, lacy midsummer blooms and long, durable stems, when grown in full sun and moderately fertile soil, with no excessive winter moisture.

Lady's mantle (Zones 4–7; 2 feet tall and 30 inches wide). Plant it in partial to full shade and well-drained soil (it is drought tolerant). It produces foamy clusters of tiny chartreuse blossoms.

'Mammoth Mid Blue' sweet peas (annual; can climb up to 6 feet high). If the summer stays cool enough, you can continue to harvest versatile sweet peas through fall. They need rich, well-drained soil and as much sun as possible.

Colewort (Zones 6–9; 8 feet tall and 5 feet wide). It needs fertile, well-drained soil and full sun to produce its strong, multibranched stems and tufts of small white flowers from late spring to midsummer.

BULBS

Are you planning out your garden for the next season? Check out these favorite bulbs and learn how to plant them properly to give your garden some real interest and beauty.

Plant a Flurry of the Hardiest Snowdrops

The most reliable species is *G. nivalis*, the common snowdrop. Although the exceptionally hardy *G. nivalis* usually flowers in March in my Zone 6 (–10°F) garden, two old English nicknames for this species, "Fair Maids of February" and "Candlemas Bells" (Candlemas falls on February 2), indicate that blossoming time may be significantly earlier under milder weather conditions. The narrow, pointed leaves, each with a hard white tip, readily push through frozen ground and snow, to be followed soon after by the dainty blossoms. Each snowy white bloom bears a cap of bright green and dangles like a single tiny lantern from a strong stem. Though small, usually ranging from 3 to 4 inches high, *G. nivalis* is good for cutting, makes an excellent candidate for miniature winter nosegays, and has a faint, honeylike scent.

Grape hyacinth (*Muscari latilfolium*)

Crocuses Can Be Spicy Autumn Bloomers

Dutch crocus (*Cronus vernus*) is the common spring-blooming species, but there are two autumn-flowering species you may want to get to know. *Crocus speciosus* bears long-tubed flowers in shades of violet-blue with deeper blue veins and divided, bright orange styles. It naturalizes easily in grass, as it increases rapidly by seeds and offsets. Saffron crocus (*Crocus sativas*), which generally will not flower in cool, wet areas, actually produces what is called the world's most expensive spice. It's obtained from the flower's long, conspicuous, deep red style. (FYI: It takes about 14,000 stigmas to make 1 ounce of saffron threads!)

—*FINE GARDENING* EDITORS

Grape Hyacinths You May Not Know

For formal plantings where you want more control, select sterile or slow-spreading varieties like *Muscari latifolium*, but choose fertile plants like 'Blue Magic' grape hyacinth for naturalizing.

Plant multiple varieties for successive blooms. *Muscari azureum* displays its sky blue flowers in early spring, followed by the fluffy heads of 'Blue Spike' grape hyacinth in mid-spring. Toward the end of the season, long-lasting dark blue 'Saffier' appears along with the feathery violet inflorescences of 'Plumosum'.

Take advantage of unusual forms and colors. The conical flowers of *Muscari paradoxum* and the broccoli-resembling blossoms of 'Fantasy Creation' provide interest, while the powder blue blossoms of 'Valerie Finnis' add stunning color to any garden.

—ILENE STERNBERG

Combine Grape Hyacinths With . . .

Tulips (*Tulipa* spp. and cvs.), daffodils (*Narcissus* spp. and cvs.), squills (*Scilla siberica* cvs.), windflowers (*Anemone blanda* cvs.), and candytufts (*Iberis sempervirens*). They also mingle well in the semi-shade with primrose (*Primula* spp. and cvs.), leopard's bane (*Doronicum* spp. and cvs.), corydalis (*Corydalis* spp. and cvs), and hellebores (*Helleborus* spp. and cvs). Or why not try them with pale-colored pinks (*Dianthus* spp. and cvs.) or species tulips, such as *Tulipa saxatilis*? Grape hyacinths show off well as filler between other plants and tucked into ground covers, and, of course, they can form a glorious field of dreams: If you plant them, they will come.

—ILENE STERNBERG

Camouflage Daffodil Foliage

Left to its own devices, daffodil foliage does take its own sweet time in going dormant, often lingering in my garden through June. As long as a daffodil's foliage is fresh and green, it is photosynthesizing and contributing to the food supply for the following season by actively storing energy in the bulb. For this reason, I plant daffodils behind groups of daylilies. The vigorous, arching foliage of the daylilies soon hides the yellowing leaves of the daffodils. Dense, bushy perennials like threadleaf coreopsis (*Coreopsis verticillata*) and catmint (*Nepeta* spp. and cvs.) can serve the same purpose. Having tucked the daffodil foliage out of sight behind the daylilies and other perennials, I rarely bother to cut it down. Every spring I mulch the perennial beds with chopped leaves, and the dead daffodil foliage becomes a component in this layer of organic mulch.

—SYDNEY EDDISON

Increase the Lifespan of Tulips

Dig holes the depth of a shovel blade (about 10 inches) and cover the bulbs with about 8 inches of soil instead of the customary 4 to 6 inches. Most mouse and vole runs are relatively shallow. It is hard to say if the deeper planting alone is protection against them, but it helps.

—SYDNEY EDDISON

Protect Tulip Bulbs from Squirrels

The only foolproof way to stop squirrels from digging up and eating your tulip bulbs is to build a chicken-

'Jeannine' golden garlic (*Allium Moly* 'Jeannine')

wire cage over the area where you've planted the bulbs. The cage muse be partially or entirely buried in the ground and must enclose the area completely. Squirrels are quite agile, so they can climb even very high fences or dive down on your garden from overhanging branches. Rodent repellents are useless, so don't waste your money on them.

—BILL QUARLES

Alliums Can Provide All-Season Color and Shape

Alliums are often overlooked as one of the best bulbs for constant color throughout the seasons. But these easy-to-grow bulbs have options that will keep the blooms coming right up to the first frost.

—STEPHANIE COHEN

Choose a Giant and a Delicate Allium for Late Spring

In late spring, **'Jeannine' golden garlic** *Allium moly* 'Jeannine', (Zones 3–9) emerges, growing a scant foot tall (see photo above). It has two stems of individual, star-shaped, golden yellow flowers forming a circular floret. To get any kind of display, plant at least a dozen bulbs. 'Jeannine' multiplies continuously and, in a few years, will put on quite a show.

—STEPHANIE COHEN

Giant Onions for Beautiful Color and Shape

Looking like a giant lollipop on a stick is the **Giant onion** *Allium giganteum* (Zones 5–9), which peeks out in late spring and grows up tall and bold. The 4-inch-diameter flower is a pretty shade of lilac, but the large leaves are troublesome, turning yellow even before full flowering is complete. But the flowers are long blooming and are excellent to use as cut flowers.

—STEPHANIE COHEN

Nod Out in Summer

Summer-flowering alliums display quite a bit of diversity. **Nodding onion**, *Allium cernuum* (Zones 4–8) is a northeastern native bulb. It gets its common name because its dainty light pink flowers hang down. Nodding onion starts flowering in early summer and has a long bloom period. Because this allium stands only 18 inches tall, it easily tucks in between spring- and summer-flowering perennials. For those who have never grown this bulb, be aware that it always nods. This does not mean it needs water.

—STEPHANIE COHEN

A Fall Allium Star

Fall is for flowers, and alliums are no exception. **'Ozawa' Japanese onion**, *Allium thunbergii* 'Ozawa' (Zones 4–9) starts to bloom in September, when most plants are winding down (but it sometimes goes to frost in my cold Zone 6). The good news is that, because it blooms so late, the shiny, narrow foliage never looks bad. The starlike purple flowers give the illusion of being large on such a small plant.

—STEPHANIE COHEN

Grow Your Own Garlic

Once you taste home-grown garlic, you won't be satisfied with supermarket varieties. Garlic isn't hard to grow. In fact, it's almost ridiculously easy. It has a few important requirements that are easily met: decent soil, adequate moisture, and, of course, planting and harvesting at the right time. Plant garlic four to six weeks before the ground freezes in your area. You can fudge the planting time a little. I have planted as early as September (by mistake) and as late as Thanksgiving (to experiment) and have had decent crops. Roots will start to grow soon after you plant. Your aim is to get good root development before the plants go dormant. Green shoots may appear in the fall, which is fine.

—RUTH LIVELY

Plant Spring-Flowering Bulbs at the Right Depth

As a rule, the proper planting depth for a spring-flowering bulb is two to three times the bulb's height. But if you'd rather skip the math, here's a quick reference for several spring favorites. Instead of digging a hole for each bulb, save time by digging holes wide enough to plant five or six at once. Grouped bulbs always look better than ones standing solo, anyway.

—ANN E. STRATTON

Giant onion
(*Allium
giganteum*)

QUICK BULB-PLANTING GUIDE

SPECIES	ZONES	DEPTH	SPACING
Crocus (*Crocus* spp. and cvs.)	3 to 8	3 inches	2 to 3 inches
Squill (*Scilla* spp. and cvs.)	4 to 9	3 to 4 inches	1 to 2 inches
Snowdrop (*Galanthus* spp. and cvs.)	3 to 9	3 to 4 inches	2 to 3 inches
Checkered lily (*Fritillaria meleagris* and cvs.)	4 to 9	5 to 6 inches	3 to 4 inches
Tulip (*Tulipa* spp. and cvs.)	4 to 8	6 to 8 inches	6 inches
Summer snowflake (*Leucojum aestivum* and cvs.)	3 to 9	4 to 6 inches	5 to 6 inches
Allium (*Allium schubertii*)	4 to 10	5 to 6 inches	4 to 5 inches
Daffodil (*Narcissus* spp. and cvs.)	3 to 9	6 inches	6 to 8 inches

ANNUALS

Old-fashioned annuals are the magic ingredients that turn a planting into something truly enchanting. Most of these old-fashioned annuals are taller than the average annuals that you'll find in garden centers today. What you get when you plant modern, already-in-bloom dwarf hybrids is a squat little display with none of the visual delight of varying heights, intermingling foliage textures, and lovely long, slender stems swaying in the breeze. You only get instant color—and instant color does not a charming garden make.

You'll most likely have to start them from seed, unless you can find small plants offered at local farmers' markets or plant sales. The good news is that these heirlooms would not have made it to modern times were they not supremely easy to grow. And because many of them self-sow reliably, you'll have lots of extra plants to fill your garden in the coming seasons.

—ANNIE HAYES

10 MUST-HAVES

1. ROSY PINK FLOWERS SWAY IN THE BREEZE

Name: 'Milas' corn cockle (*Agrostemma githago* 'Milas')
Size: Up to 3 feet tall and 18 inches wide
Conditions: Full sun; rich, well-drained soil
Best way to grow: Sow seeds outdoors as soon as the weather begins to warm up, or buy small plants to set out after the last frost date. Transplant carefully without disturbing the roots.

'Milas' corn cockle is my favorite cottage-garden classic. It's easy to grow and delivers the ultimate in charm. Upright, slender stems sway gracefully with the slightest breeze, topped by elegant, satiny, bright rose blooms, each with a delicate pattern of radiating black dotted lines. It produces up to 100 blooms at a time, making it a perfect cut flower. It self-sows, too—plant one this year and you'll get 10 or more fresh new plants next spring. This is a spring bloomer that will last for about a month and a half, although it will keep going into summer and fall in places where summers are cool. Slugs and snails are attracted to this plant, so plan accordingly.

2. A COLOR THAT GOES WITH EVERYTHING

Name: 'Lime Green' flowering tobacco (*Nicotiana alata* 'Lime Green', tall form)
Size: Up to 3 feet tall and 1 to 2 feet wide
Conditions: Full sun to partial shade; rich, moist, well-drained soil
Best way to grow: Surface-sow seeds indoors in early spring and set out seedlings after the last frost date, or buy small plants. Do not allow seedlings to dry out.

Once upon a time, not too long ago, flowering tobaccos were 3 feet tall or more. Then breeders decided that the plants should be only 1 foot tall so that growers could sell them already blooming in a pot. It is amazing how quickly the original and more garden-worthy forms have been forgotten. I often use the properly-3-foot-tall 'Lime Green' flowering tobacco in my gardens. It goes with everything and every color, and it seems to make any plant I combine with it pop. Tough and adaptable, it blooms for many months. In coastal California, it can grow in sun or shade, although it is usually grown everywhere else in bright shade, where its greeny green color is most radiant. After it has finished blooming, all you need to do is cut it back to about 5 inches tall and it will quickly bloom again. This plant acts as a long-blooming perennial in temperate climates and self-sows reliably every season elsewhere.

3. A RAINBOW OF COLORS FROM AN EASY-TO-GROW VINE

Name: Spanish flag (*Mina lobata*)
Size: Climbing up to 10 feet
Conditions: Full sun; rich, moist, well-drained soil
Best way to grow: Sow seeds outdoors in late spring, or buy small plants to set out after the last frost date.

The startling, triple-toned flower spikelets of this old-fashioned vine, also known as exotic love vine, never fail to amaze those who see it for the first time. This vigorous member of the morning glory family bears attractive, good-size, lush, fleur de lis–shaped foliage thick enough to blanket a chain-link fence. It bursts into a mass of blooms for several months, starting in midsummer. Beginning at the base, the blooms start out primrose yellow and shift to peach, orange, and scarlet, with all the colors appearing simultaneously. Spanish flag is incredibly easy to grow. It helps to place it where the base of the plant will get shade. This is a terrific choice for an arbor or trellis. Plant three under a tall obelisk in a large container for a magnificent display. It usually self-sows, so you'll have it again the following year.

4. A LUSH VERSION OF A CALIFORNIA CLASSIC

Name: 'Apricot Chiffon' California poppy (*Eschscholzia californica* 'Apricot Chiffon')

Size: Up to 14 inches tall and wide

Conditions: Full sun; rich, moist, well-drained soil; drought tolerant

Best way to grow: Sow seeds outdoors as soon as the weather warms up, or buy small plants to set out after the last frost date. Transplant carefully without disturbing the roots.

No matter where you plant this gorgeous poppy in your garden, you'll love it. Its fluted, 2- to 3-inch-wide peachy flowers are true eye candy. The blue-green foliage creates a feathery mound that is best used at the front of the garden, where it won't be crowded out by taller plants and where it can soften the edge of a bed. It blooms for a month or more, and you can easily extend the bloom by deadheading it. Not too fussy about soil or water, 'Apricot Chiffon' is certainly most glorious in rich, well-drained soil and average moisture. It self-sows to return each spring but will revert to the more dominant orange color if there are any of those in the neighborhood that the bees might visit.

5. A FRESH LOOK TO MASK THE BARE KNEES OF OTHER PLANTS

Name: 'Blue Pearl' German catchfly (*Lychnis viscaria* 'Blue Pearl', syn. *Viscaria oculata* 'Blue Pearl')

Size: 2 feet tall and 20 inches wide

Conditions: Full sun; rich, moist, well-drained soil

Best way to grow: Because seeds for this tall variety are not commercially available, you'll have to buy small plants to set out after the last frost date.

'Blue Pearl' German catchfly is another many-stemmed, gracefully balletic heirloom dishing up a multitude of more-than-lovely lavender-blue flowers. The color is sublime, and its ever-bobbing blossoms look wonderful, both mid-bed and right up front. Because it's a fast grower, with low, grasslike foliage, you can plant it in front of dahlias and taller perennials whose lower stems and foliage you'd like to disguise.

6. DRAPING RIBBONS OF PINK FOR THE FRONT OR BACK OF A BORDER

Name: Kiss-me-over-the-garden-gate (*Polygonum orientale*, syn. *Persicaria orientalis*)

Size: Up to 8 feet tall and 2 feet wide

Conditions: Full sun; rich, moist, well-drained soil

Best way to grow: Sow seeds outdoors as soon as the weather warms up, or buy small plants to set out after the last frost date.

If you haven't yet grown old-timey kiss-me-over-the-garden-gate, you must—at the very least for its wonderfully nostalgic name. This fast-growing member of the knotweed family will reach 6 feet tall in a month. Loads of showy, 4-inch-long flower heads, which look like dense, beaded clusters, arch out in all directions on strong, upright, branching stems. The large, heart-shaped, tropical-looking leaves are showy, too, and extend to the base, so you don't get a bare-bottom look. This showstopper is gratifying wherever you plant it. It's great behind roses and toward the back of a bed, but it's also a delightful surprise right up front, where everyone will want to know what it is. This plant tolerates lots of heat and humidity, and it self-sows reliably.

7. A DRAMATIC COMBO OF RED AND BLACK

Name: 'Ladybird' poppy (*Papaver commutatum* 'Ladybird')
Size: 12 to 16 inches tall and wide
Conditions: Full sun; rich, moist, well-drained soil
Best way to grow: Sow seeds outdoors as soon as the weather warms up, or buy small plants to set out after the last frost date. Transplant carefully without disturbing the roots.

Nothing adds dazzle to a spring garden like this brilliant, true red poppy. Everyone loves its vivid blooms, but it's also popular because of its neat and tidy habit. Each compact mound of bright green foliage displays fifteen to twenty 3-inch-wide blooms at a time. This plant is especially stunning when planted throughout a garden; when it blooms, you'll want to have a party. It also makes a marvelous container plant. 'Ladybird' blooms for at least a month, and if you deadhead, you can extend the bloom season for a month or more. This poppy, unfortunately, does not self-sow—at least not in California. Poppies are best planted out early, right after the last frost date.

8. CONFETTI FOR THE GARDEN

Name: Multicolored flowering tobacco (*Nicotiana mutabilis*)
Size: 5 to 6 feet tall and 4 feet wide
Conditions: Light to partial shade; rich, moist, well-drained soil
Best way to grow: Surface-sow seeds indoors in early spring and set out seedlings after the last frost date, or buy small plants. Do not allow seedlings to dry out.

The lesser-known multicolored flowering tobacco blooms for months, thrilling us with three different colors of flowers—all at the same time. One-inch-wide bright rose, soft pink, and white blooms are held in a multistemmed, 4-foot-wide, bouncing cloud. Fun, fascinating, and colorful, it's a welcome choice for a bright- or partial-shade garden, and it looks great with blue hydrangeas. Cut it back to 5 inches tall after it finally peters out and it will happily rebloom, especially if you ply it with a little compost. It readily self-sows and is a favorite treat for hummingbirds but not snails or deer.

9. THIS VINE WILL HAVE EVERYONE TALKING

Name: Monjita (*Scyphanthus elegans*)
Size: Climbing up to 8 feet
Conditions: Full sun; rich, moist, well-drained soil
Best way to grow: This plant is rare in the trade and challenging to grow from seed. Mail-order small plants to set out after the last frost date.

Monjita is one of our most fascinating annual discoveries of the past few years. This nimble climber from Chile begins blooming within a month after being planted from a 4-inch-diameter container and continues for up to four months. Its refined, lacy foliage clings to any support you provide and soon bears a slew of intriguing, sunny yellow flowers. Jutting out from the center of the pleated blooms are prominent, shiny red structures, which I can only assume are meant to attract pollinators. This plant is easy, fast growing, and rewarding, and it's great for when you need something new and different to elevate your gardener's curiosity.

10. A BRIGHT-EYED SPILLER THAT'S ALSO A NATIVE

Name: Baby blue-eyes (*Nemophila menziesii* and cvs.)
Size: 10 to 12 inches tall and 20 inches wide
Conditions: Full sun; rich, moist, well-drained soil
Best way to grow: Sow seeds indoors in early spring, or buy small plants to set out after the last frost date. Put out bait for snails, and protect plants from birds.

This romantic, melt-your-heart, true-blue trailer bubbles and spills beautifully over the edges of garden beds for several months. To grow it is to love it. One of our favorite California native annuals, baby blue-eyes forms a spreading mound covered with color-of-the-sky flowers all spring and into summer. Plant baby blue-eyes early: as soon as the threat of frost is over in cold winter areas and no later than mid-February in areas with mild winters. It's excellent in containers, and it self-sows, too. Just watch out for those slugs.

Six Things You Need to Know About Geraniums

—RICHARD HAWKE

1. Don't get them confused with their cousins. True geraniums (*Geranium* spp. and cvs.) are often referred to as "hardy geraniums" to distinguish them from their tender cousins: the colorful bedding (or zonal) geraniums (*Pelargonium* spp. and cvs.). An alternate common name of true geraniums, cranesbill, is a nod to their slender fruit, which resembles the beak of a crane.

2. The foliage can be as cool as the flowers. Most geraniums have attractive foliage, and although quite variable, their leaves are generally lobed and often deeply dissected. Leaf colors range from bright green to gray-green, but there are a number of varieties that have purple, bronze, or yellow leaves. Many, however, don't hold their foliage color throughout the season. We had the best success with the Victor Reiter strain, a seed strain of meadow geranium (*G. pratense*) that loses its deep purple leaf color in midsummer but turns purple again in fall.

3. Trim them back for a better habit. Although geraniums are not high-maintenance plants, most must be cut back after flowering. Shearing stems back to new basal leaves reins in unruly habits and rejuvenates plants to an almost springlike quality. Deadheading also reduces self-seeding, which can be excessive.

4. Color doesn't end when the flowers do. Come autumn, many geraniums turn shades of purple, red, orange, or yellow—and often on the same plant. Cambridge geranium and bigroot geranium are among my picks for the best autumnal displays.

5. They're not picky about conditions. Geraniums are generally easy to grow in a variety of light conditions from full sun to full shade and in most soils, except those that are overly wet or too dry. Rich, moist soil is ideal for most geraniums—even drought-tolerant species, such as bigroot geranium. Morning sun will encourage stronger habits and better flower production on shade-loving geraniums and will enhance leaf color on bronze-leaved forms, like 'Elizabeth Ann' and 'Espresso'. In hot regions, afternoon shade is priceless for keeping geraniums happy and healthy.

6. Pests and diseases plague only some types. Geraniums are rarely troubled by diseases or pests, but powdery mildew, leaf spotting, rabbits, and Japanese beetles are occasional problems. Powdery mildew is notable on cultivars of meadow geraniums only, while Japanese beetles find the many cultivars of Druce's geranium (*G. oxonianum*) delectable. And mourning widow geraniums, especially 'Margaret Wilson', prove to be irresistibly succulent treats for rabbits.

HYDRANGEAS

Choose a Cold-Hardy Cultivar

Researchers like Dr. Sandra Reed, research geneticist at the United States National Arboretum, and the staff at North Carolina State University's Mountain Horticultural Crops Research and Extension Center, in Fletcher, have been evaluating hundreds of hydrangea cultivars for cold hardiness. After five years of research in test plots in Missouri (Zone 5), Tennessee (Zone 6), and North Carolina (Zone 7), these are among the selections we found to have the most consistent flowers for areas with cold winter temperatures. All are hardy in Zones 5 to 9.

have relatively large and abundant flowers that repeat in autumn, but they've won me over for their reliability under diverse conditions.

If pink mopheads are more your style, 'Glowing Embers' (syn. 'Alpenglühen' and 'Alpenglow') is the best reddish pink variety I saw in the bunch. 'Masja' was a close second, with its compact habit and attractive hot pink flowers. But for those gardeners who prefer white flowers, I highly recommend 'Madame Emile Mouillère'. Alas, this pure white cultivar is not reliably hardy for us in the exposed southern Blue Ridge Mountains, but in a sheltered site it is a precious gem.

'Nikko Blue' hydrangea (*Hydrangea macrophylla* 'Nikko Blue')

Mopheads provide showy flowers. One of the best blue-flowering mopheads by far is 'All Summer Beauty'. Its sky blue blossoms open with a white eye that matures to all blue. 'Nikko Blue', a variety with clear blue flowers, is also an outstanding shrub. Both

'Glowing Embers' hydrangea (*Hydrangea macrophylla* 'Glowing Ebers')

Lacecaps have a delicate form. 'Bluebird' and 'Tokyo Delight' both produce lovely, flat, doilylike blossoms and are wonderfully dependable. 'Tokyo Delight' has large pale blue or pink flowers that fade to nearly white, while 'Bluebird' displays totally blue blooms above its attractive and vigorous foliage. When the flowers of 'Bluebird' set seed, the sterile florets turn upward, revealing their pink undersides regardless of the soil pH.

—DICK BIR

HOW TO GO FROM PINK TO BLUE TO PINK

SOIL CONDITION	COLOR	TO CHANGE COLOR
Acidic soil with aluminum	Blue flowers	Add lime and phosphorus to raise the pH and block aluminum uptake.
Alkaline soil with aluminum	Pink flowers	Add organic matter like compost or composted manure around the base of the plant to lower the pH.
Acidic soil with no aluminum	Pink flowers	Add aluminum sulfate to increase aluminum content.
Alkaline soil with no aluminum	Pink flowers	Add aluminum sulfate to lower the pH and increase aluminum content.

—DICK BIR

Avoid Too Much Shade

Two words to remember when it comes to hydrangeas that refuse to flower are *too much.* Bigleaf hydrangeas grow well in the shade in most areas of the United States; however, too much shade can result in gorgeous leaves and no flowers. The high shade created by deciduous trees or evergreens is perfect for bigleaf hydrangeas in the East, Midwest, and Northwest. In California, any shade you can find, as long as it is not too dense, seems to work. But hydrangeas located near a foggy coast and in northern areas of the country require no shade at all.

—DICK BIR

Go Easy With the Fertilizer

A high-nitrogen fertilizer will result in beautiful leaves and few, if any, flowers. Bigleaf hydrangeas can tolerate very high levels of fertilizer without showing signs of fertilizer burn, so practice moderation. Too much water and too much dryness can also result in a lack of flowers.

—DICK BIR

Plant Placement Protects Flower Buds from the Cold

Cold winter temperatures can often kill off flower buds. This problem can be addressed by planting bigleaf hydrangeas on north- or east-facing slopes rather than toward the south or west, which are the first areas to warm up in late winter, triggering buds to open too early. Choosing cold-hardy varieties and siting plants under a canopy of evergreen trees can help to avoid winter kill.

—DICK BIR

Change Your Soil pH to Change Bloom Color

The flowers of bigleaf hydrangeas are blue in very acidic soil and pink in slightly acidic soil. The color comes from anthocyanins, which are water-soluble pigments within plant cells that appear blue when stacked close together and pink when farther apart.

The effect of soil acidity on blossom colors is actually indirect. Aluminum is responsible for changing the hues of hydrangeas, allowing anthocyanin molecules to move closer together, resulting in blue coloration. It becomes more soluble in acidic soil and, therefore, is more readily absorbed by plants.

—LEE REICH

Acidity Levels Also Affect Other Flowers

Soil acidity and the resulting aluminum uptake could also affect the pink-to-blue color change with other flowers. Some flowers, such as wild morning glories, are pink when they initially unfold and then turn blue. Why? No one knows. But aluminum is toxic to plants, and death usually results at levels needed to effect that color change. Even hydrangeas are not immune to aluminum toxicity, so keep tabs on soil acidity. To maintain blue hydrangeas, a pH of 5.0 to 5.5 is ideal.

—LEE REICH

Winter Care

- **Occasional applications of compost** forked into the soil will give your hydrangeas an excellent environment for root development.

- **A year-round mulch** will also help maintain moisture and evenness of ground temperature.

- **Use a balanced fertilizer high in nitrogen** during the active growing season, then taper off the nitrogen and provide only phosphorus and potassium toward bloom time.

- **As winter approaches**, mound up fir branches, straw, or whatever you can find, or build a cylindrical shelter from stakes and burlap to keep in place until all danger of frost has passed. This extra protection will prevent or diminish winterkill and assure you of beautiful blossoms next summer.

—KEITH DAVITT

Cut the Confusion

The three most common reasons that people are confused about when to prune hydrangeas are the plant's dead-looking appearance in winter, its failure to bloom in summer, and the reasoning that because it's a shrub it needs to be pruned. But these popular woody plants can live long, floriferous lives without ever feeling the cold blade of a pair of Felcos. Hydrangeas, though, can handle pruning (which, if done at the wrong time, may be the cause for the

lack of flowers), and sometimes you might want or need to cut them back a bit. Pruning hydrangeas can also improve a shrub's vigor and increase the size of its flowers.

—JANET CARSON

Distinguish Between Old and New Wood

Not all of these shrubs should be pruned at the same time. Those that bloom on old growth should only be pruned after flowering. Others bloom on new growth and should be pruned before they wake up in spring or as they are going dormant in fall.

—JANET CARSON

Prune Blooms on Old Wood

To determine if your hydrangea blooms on old wood, think about when it flowers. Shrubs with this characteristic generally begin blooming in early summer and peter out by midsummer, though sporadic blooms may appear afterward. These shrubs form next year's flower buds in late summer or early fall as the days get shorter and temperatures cool off. To reduce the risk of removing these buds, prune just as the flowers begin to fade. Often, the earlier you get it done after bloom, the quicker the shrub can recover, producing more and larger blooms next season.

- **Don't prune these hydrangeas to the ground in late fall.** Doing so removes all of next year's flower buds.

- **To tidy up, remove old blooms.** Gardeners who want to maintain a tidy appearance can snip off spent blooms just below the flower head and remove any wayward or straggly canes at the soil line.

- **To improve vigor, remove the oldest canes.** When a hydrangea gets old and woody, it can produce smaller blooms. Regular removal of a few of the oldest canes at the soil line can keep the shrub vigorous, producing large and abundant flowers. The same method can keep a shrub from getting too tall by targeting the tallest canes for removal.

—JANET CARSON

Prune Blooms on New Wood

Because they need to grow and set buds the same year that they bloom, shrubs that flower on new wood generally start blossoming later than old-growth bloomers, beginning in midsummer and continuing until the first frost. These shrubs are forgiving if pruning is not done at a certain time as long as you avoid pruning when the flower buds are opening.

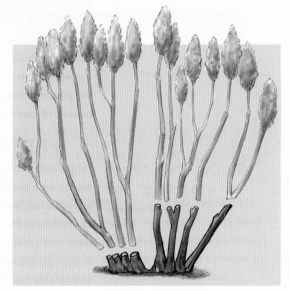

- **To get bigger flowers, cut them all the way back.** In late winter or early spring, these shrubs can be cut all the way back to the ground. Smooth hydrangeas will produce much larger blooms if pruned hard like this each year, but many gardeners opt for smaller blooms on sturdier stems.

—JANET CARSON

Sow Peas in Bands, Not in Rows
—DAVID HIRSCH

I've found that peas help keep each other propped up if they are planted close together. For dwarf varieties (those that grow less than 3 feet tall), I scatter the seeds an inch or two apart in a 6-inch-wide band, and cover them with ½ inch of soil. As they grow, the plants' tendrils wrap around each other, and the whole clump stays off the ground.

Keep the Basil Coming
—SUSAN BELSINGER

Prune basil early.

Basil is an easy plant to grow, its only major requirements being full sun and consistent water. It is important to keep basils cut back so that you have a continual harvest of fresh leaves throughout the season. I am diligent about pruning my plants, and as a result I get 15 to 25 cups of leaves from each plant per season. It is also important not to let the plants slated for culinary use flower, or the leaves will begin to taste bitter.

Immediately after planting, I prune my basils by cutting them back to just above the bottom two sets of leaves. This early pruning may seem drastic, but it actually stimulates growth. Depending on the weather and how quickly the plants are growing, I prune the plants back again to just above the bottom two sets of leaves about every four weeks, or sooner if they show any sign of flowering.

Grow (and Contain) Mint
—RON ZIMMERMAN

No kitchen garden should be without at least a few mint plants. For drinks or desserts, or to pair with savory foods, mint's clean and bracing flavor has earned it a place in many recipes. But mint is never content to stay put, and it can be one of the most invasive plants in the garden. So to avoid starting an herbal jungle, you'll want to keep mint in check. Because mints cross and hybridize easily, it is best to propagate them by taking cuttings, dividing roots, or buying plants rather than starting them from seed.

At our farm, we curtail mint's invasive habit by planting it in terracotta chimney-flue liners. These can be set directly on the ground or partially buried, and because they have no bottoms, drainage isn't a problem. By playing around with their placement, you can add architectural interest and charm to your garden.

Flue liners are available from building or masonry suppliers. They are 1 foot square and 2 feet long, but they can be shortened using a circular saw with a masonry blade. Like most terra-cotta, the flue liners can spall—that is, they flake off in pieces with repeated exposure to rain, snow, and freezing. Our liners usually last five to eight years before their antique charm seems excessive.

Let Chard Take You Past the First Frost

—LAURA MCGRATH

Chard makes the late-summer garden look lush, even when the tomatoes are devastated by wilt and the beans are disappearing under hordes of Mexican bean beetles. Unlike many greens, chard will produce steadily through the hottest days of summer and the first autumn frosts. If you pick the outer stalks, new ones will emerge. So direct-sow the seeds in spring. And while chard makes few demands as it grows, the key to vigorous mature plants is regular watering when the plants are small.

GROW THE THREE SISTERS TOGETHER

There is so much to learn from Native American agricultural practices. The Iroquois' staple crops were the three sisters: corn, beans, and squash. They planted them together because these crops were thought to be the sustainers of life. To this day, one of the most successful ways to grow beans is by using the three sisters concept.

1. **Plant the corn** after the last day of frost. Build a mound about 1 foot high and between 1½ and 3 feet in diameter. Sow four corn seeds 6 inches apart in the center of the mound.

2. **Plant the beans** once the corn is 4 inches tall. Sow four bean seeds 3 inches away from the corn plants.

3. **Plant the squash.** Sow four seeds, about a foot away from the beans, eventually thinning them down to one. If you are planting a large area, you can also sow the squash in separate mounds (1 foot in diameter) between every few corn and bean mounds.

The corn serves as a pole for your beans to climb. Beans, like other legumes, have bacteria living on their roots that help them absorb nitrogen from the air and convert it to a form that plants can use. Corn, which requires a lot of nitrogen to grow, benefits the most. The bean vines also provide extra rigidity, preventing the corn stalk from falling down during windy or rainy days. The squash provides a layer of shade at soil level, keeping the weeds down and the moisture up.

—PATTI MORENO

THE BEST HEIRLOOM VEGETABLES

Gardeners sometimes think that heirloom varieties are more susceptible to pests and diseases because, unlike many hybrids, they weren't specially bred to resist these threats. This isn't necessarily true. Heirloom varieties that are grown in the same location year after year will, in fact, naturally adapt to regional conditions, making them a hedge against pests, diseases, and changing environmental conditions. Of the hundreds of heirlooms that I've grown, these eight varieties have become regular fixtures in my USDA Hardiness Zone 4 garden, selected for their superb taste and ease of growing.

—JOHN TORGRIMSON

'Dragon' carrot

What's not to love about the bright red-purple skin of this attractive heirloom? Don't be surprised, though, when you cut into the spears and find a yellow-orange interior. Like most carrots, well-drained soil is a must. To ensure good drainage, I plant 'Dragon' in an old livestock water tank (but any large container or pot would work) that's filled with compost-amended soil. The sweet, slightly spicy flavor is best enjoyed when the carrots are roasted with other vegetables, like potatoes, beets, squash, peppers, onions, and garlic.

Days to maturity: 90

'Gold Medal' tomato

I grow six to eight different heirloom tomato varieties each year—from cherries to slicers to canners. 'Gold Medal', a fist-size, orange-red beefsteak, is my "sit-down-in-the-garden-and-eat-it-right-now" favorite. When I am able to display some degree of discipline, I eat it sliced on toast with a dash of olive oil and basil on top. This moderate-yield tomato is, for me, the singular taste of summer. Start the indeterminate plants inside, and transplant them as soon as the threat of frost has passed.

Days to maturity: 75 to 90

'Early Scarlet Globe' radish

Spinach and radishes are the first things I harvest each spring, and this variety is one of the earliest to mature. Direct-sow the seed when the ground is workable, regardless of whether the last frost of spring has occurred. The 1-inch-diameter globes have a bright red skin and white flesh, and although I associate planting and eating radishes with a new spring garden, this variety can also be grown in fall. I like to serve 'Early Scarlet Globe' sliced and mixed into salads.

Days to maturity: 20 to 28

'Rattlesnake' snap bean

This bean gets its name from the dark purple streaks on its skin, which resemble the markings on a rattlesnake (the stripes magically go away, though, when you cook them). This variety is a vigorous climber that can reach 10 feet tall, so it requires some heavy-duty support. Other than needing something to climb on, 'Rattlesnake' snap bean requires minimal care and has good drought resistance. The beans taste great at any time of the year. I especially like freezing them, then adding them to soups in January to get a taste of summer in the dead of winter.

Days to maturity: 60 to 90

'Japanese Climbing' cucumber

Last year, I picked cucumbers from this plant well into late fall. Because it's an abundant producer, be sure to check for fruit every other day when the plant is in full production. 'Japanese Climbing' cucumber is vigorous with strong grasping tendrils, so I grow it on both sides of a vertical fence to keep it off the ground. You can let the vines trail on the ground, but be sure to space the plants at least 6 feet apart. The fruit is tender, crisp, and slightly tart, and it can grow up to 9 inches long. Eat it raw, paired with tomatoes, or in summer salads; for a nice surprise, try it lightly stir-fried in your Asian dishes.

Days to maturity: 58 to 65

'Jimmy Nardello' pepper

This family heirloom originated in the Basilicata region of Italy. 'Jimmy Nardello' produces a steady flow of 10-inch-long green and red peppers, with the fruit sometimes developing into a corkscrew shape. Our family will roast this mild, sweet-flavored pepper with other vegetables or serve it stir-fried. Start the seeds inside and then transfer the plants to the garden after the last frost in spring.

Days to maturity: 80 to 90

'Mountain Rose' potato

Most fruit in the garden is visible for all to see, so there is something mysterious in turning over a forkful of soil and discovering underground bounty— in this case, a medium-size, purple-and-red-skinned potato. 'Mountain Rose' is a high-yielding, versatile variety, suitable for frying and roasting, and it works well in any potato salad. The tubers also retain their rose color after cooking. I plant rows of 'Mountain Rose' in loose, well-drained soil and cover them with straw mulch. As the plant develops, I add additional mulch for water retention and weed suppression.

Days to maturity: 70 to 90

'German Extra Hardy' garlic

Two years ago, I grew 8,000 heads of garlic to sell as seed, and of those varieties, 'German Extra Hardy' was (and still is) my favorite. A hard-neck type, it grows good-size heads with four to seven thumb-size cloves apiece. This vigorous grower has long roots, which enable it to overwinter without heaving out of the ground. Plant the cloves after the first frost in fall, then mulch heavily. You will be able to harvest when the green plants start to yellow the following summer. The cloves have a strong flavor when raw and are great for roasting. We now grow about 400 heads of garlic each year, knowing that about 100 of the best bulbs will be used as seed (each clove becomes a seed that can grow a new bulb).

Days to maturity: 90 to 150

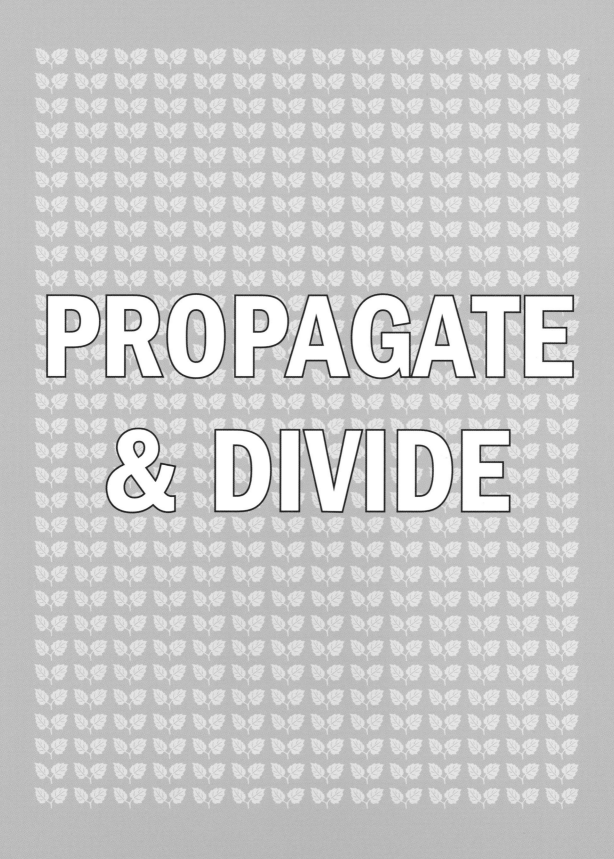

PROPAGATE
& DIVIDE

SEED STARTING

Choose Seeds of Varieties That Will Do Well in Your Area
—JANIE MALLOY

Ask friends, neighbors, and county extension agents for their recommendations. Then, buy some tried-and-true varieties, but do some experimenting, too. Just remember: If you plan to save the seeds from your plants from year to year, be sure to select seeds described as open pollinated or heirloom. Seeds from a hybrid, which is the result of crossing two plants, will not produce the same plant from year to year.

Control Seed Flow with a Hand Sower
—FINE GARDENING EDITORS

Anyone who has ever tried to evenly distribute carrot seeds when planting—and has gone cross-eyed trying to do it—will appreciate this practical tool. A hand seed sower allows you to load a packet of seeds and control their flow rate through different-size outlets, ensuring your crops will always be evenly spaced. The funnel-shaped end also makes it easy to return any unused seeds back to the packet.

Start Your Seeds Indoors
—JANIE MALLOY

Plan to start your seeds indoors so that they are at the proper stage of development to set outside at the optimal time. For northern gardeners, this is crucial because the growing season is short and good

timing increases your production. For mild-weather gardeners, it can mean getting two or three crops (of corn, for instance) in a season by removing the remnants of a harvested crop and planting three-week-old seedlings in their place. Perfecting this technique requires good timing and seed selection, understanding your climate and soil, and some practice in starting seedlings.

Pick Containers That Have Drainage Holes

—JANIE MALLOY

You'll need containers that have drainage holes and a tray or something to catch excess water. Old plastic six-packs or 4-inch-tall containers work well. Styrofoam cups and plastic tubs are great for sharing seedlings with friends. You can also buy a gadget that compresses soil into blocks or one that molds newspaper into little biodegradable pots. Peat pots tend to restrict the progress of the seedlings' roots; peat pellets work a little better. Just be aware that organic pots dry quickly and need to be watched. My favorite tray is a foil baking dish with holes poked in the bottom, with another one underneath to catch excess water. Whatever you use, be sure to clean and sterilize it. Wash recycled containers in a weak solution of laundry bleach to sterilize.

Store Your Seeds in a Cool, Dry, Dark Place

—BRANDI SPADE

Seeds don't last forever. If you're buying seeds rather than saving your own, check for an expiration or sell-by date. Don't buy seeds if the date has passed or is right around the corner. When saving your own seeds, make sure to let the seeds dry out before storing them. Store seeds in a cool, dark, dry place; an envelope of seeds in an airtight tin tucked in the back of your refrigerator is a good option. Throw in a silica-gel pack (like the one you find in vitamin bottles) to absorb moisture.

Give Larger Seeds a Nick

—SALLY ROTH

Scarification means nicking the seed coat with a knife or sandpaper so that life-giving moisture can reach the seed's embryo. If a seed is big, and I can't dent it with a fingernail, I give it the knife. A small, sharp, pocketknife blade or a rattail file is ideal. Don't go at it too zealously; you need to remove only a very small slice or section of seed coat. You can also line a jar with a sheet of sandpaper cut to fit, screw on the lid, and shake the jar like a maraca until the seed coats are abraded. Scarify seeds just before planting. Seeds nicked too long before planting may dry out and be worthless when they finally reach the soil.

Keep Them Warm
—JANIE MALLOY

Place freshly planted containers on a heated seed-starting mat or in a warm spot in the house. Individual varieties have different temperature requirements for germination. Some seed packets supply this information, but most seeds germinate between 60°F and 80°F. Seeds germinate at warmer temperatures than those needed by seedlings for growth. So after the sprouts have true leaves, you can move them to a cooler home. Some seeds need light to germinate, so check the packet for this information, too.

Remember that warmth can reduce moisture, so check the soil daily. Setting the container in direct sunlight will also dry out the potting medium. Letting the potting mix dry out or allowing the soil temperatures to fluctuate widely will reduce your germination rate. If you must water freshly planted seeds from the top, do so gently; it's preferable to watering from the bottom.

....

Turn On the Light
—JANIE MALLOY

When growing seedlings indoors, you have two choices: natural or artificial light. Seedlings need a lot of light, and spindly growth will tell you if they're not getting enough. Incandescent lights won't do because they don't provide the full spectrum of light that growing plants need. Grow lights or fluorescent lights are best. Place seedlings under them for 12 to 16 hours a day. If exposed for longer than that, the plant won't go through the metabolic processes required for growth. The key to using lights is positioning the plants at the right distance from the source: nearly touching when the plants have newly emerged, increasing later to 4 inches away.

....

Give Transplants a Drink
—SALLY ROTH

Water your plants well before transplanting them, and water the garden soil until it's well moistened but not sopping wet. Slide the plants out of their pots and into place, firm the soil around each with your fingers, and water with a fine mist. Be sure to keep the soil moist until the plants start growing well.

....

Give Seedlings Some Teatime

—IRENE MORETTI

When starting my own plants from seeds, I've always used a chemical fungicide to prevent damping off. But because it's rather expensive, I decided to try an alternative. While looking through my herb reference books, I discovered that chamomile is said to have fungicidal properties. So I emptied the contents of four organic chamomile tea bags into a quart of boiling water and allowed it to cool. I then watered one of my seedling trays with it. It worked.

That seedling tray did just as well as the ones I watered with the chemical-fungicide solution. And chamomile tea is a lot cheaper than the commercial product.

GIVE YOUR SEEDS THE SPROUTING TEST

1. Place some—not all—seeds on a moist paper towel, and cover them with another moist paper towel.

2. Put them in a plastic zip-top bag, and set the bag in a warm place.

3. Check on it often, and mist when necessary to make sure the paper towels stay moist.

4. Within a few days, most seeds should start sprouting. If few or no seeds have sprouted within two to three weeks (check seed packages for germination times), it's safe to discard the expired seeds and the remainder of the seed packet.

HARDWOOD CUTTINGS

Taking hardwood cuttings is the way to make more of your most treasured woody plants.
It's surprisingly simple. Just follow these step-by-step methods.

—DANIELLE SHERRY

Prep Work: Cut, Coat, Then Make the Mix

1. For each of the propagation methods, take cuttings of your tree or shrub in the dormant season. Cut a 6- to 8-inch-long section of stem, preferably from the previous season's growth. The top of the section should have an angled cut (to prevent water from settling and causing tip rot) just above a single bud or pair of buds. The bottom of the section should have a straight cut just below a single bud or pair of buds.

2. Dip the base of each cutting into a rooting-hormone powder, which can be found at most garden-supply stores.

3. If you are going to pot up your cuttings or put them into plastic rolls to root them, you'll need to make a special potting soil. The mixture should be 4 parts compost (peat-free) to 1 part perlite. Be sure to combine the ingredients thoroughly.

Method 1: Roll Them Up in Plastic to Make the Most Plants

1. To make the largest number of new plants in the smallest amount of space, cut a piece of black plastic that is 1 foot wide and 3 feet long; heavy-duty contractor's garbage bags work well, as do recycled potting-soil bags. Place several handfuls of moistened potting mix down the length of the plastic sheet, then line up the cuttings (2 to 3 inches apart) on top of the soil.

2. Fold in the base of the plastic sheet so that it covers the bottom 2 or 3 inches of the cuttings, then roll up the entire sheet. Secure the roll with large rubber bands, and poke drainage holes into the base with a razor blade.

3. Place the roll in a cold frame or a protected place outside, such as a spot next to the foundation of your house. When warm weather sets in and rainfall has been sparse, you can dunk the entire roll in a bucket of water occasionally to prevent the cuttings from shriveling up. Unroll the package in late summer, and replant the rooted cuttings.

Method 2: Put Them in a Pot to Get the Best Root Development

1. Fill a 1-gallon pot with potting soil and then push five to seven cuttings into the pot (around the edge), leaving just one bud or one pair of the buds exposed.

2. Water the cuttings in, making sure that the soil is consistently moist throughout the pot.

3. Place the pot in a cold frame or in an unheated location where it will still receive some light (by a window in the garage, for example), and keep it there throughout the winter and into spring. Keep the soil fairly dry during the coldest months. Increase watering as the days get warmer, and move the pot outside to a partially shaded spot after the last frost. You should see some shoot growth by mid-spring, but wait until late summer before transplanting the rooted cuttings.

Method 3: Sink Them Into the Soil to Let Nature Do the Work

1. Select a location that has amended, well-drained soil, such as a raised bed. Insert the cuttings into the soil, leaving a pair of buds aboveground and spacing them at 4- to 6-inch intervals. If the soil is partially frozen and difficult to work, use a shovel or pitchfork to dig a shallow trench.

2. Cover the cuttings with a floating row cover to help them overwinter outside without damage. Periodically check the cuttings to make sure they haven't shifted and to lightly water if the conditions are dry.

3. Remove the cover in spring, when you start to see sprouting. Wait until late summer or early fall before transplanting the rooted cuttings.

SOFTWOOD CUTTINGS

Turn Summer Cuttings Into Shrubs

—SUSAN GRILLO

Harvest Cuttings from Semi-Ripe Growth

The trickiest part of propagating shrubs from softwood cuttings is knowing when a shrub's stems are ready to be cut. Softwood, the section of a shrub's stem that's neither brand-new nor fully mature, is the stage of growth on a deciduous woody plant that is best suited for rooting. The newer, green growth that lies at the end of the stem will rot before roots are produced, and the older, woodier growth at the base of the stem has a harder time putting out roots.

Softwood cuttings can be taken from most deciduous shrubs in June and July and sometimes into early August. Determine a stem's maturity by taking it in your hand and bending it. If the stem breaks with a characteristic snapping sound, it is in the softwood stage and ready to be harvested as a cutting. If the stem is still too green, it will bend but not break. If the stem is entering the woody stage, it won't bend at all.

The best time to take cuttings is early in the day, when shoots are fully hydrated. Lateral shoots, or those that grow from a leader, make the best cuttings. As soon as you take a cutting, nestle it into a plastic basin that you've filled with damp paper towels. The towels will keep the cuttings moist and cool until you're ready to pot them up. They also

These hydrangea cuttings should form roots in fewer than six weeks.

shade cuttings from the sun. Exposure to direct sunlight, even for only a few minutes, can cause irreparable damage. Avoid taking cuttings on hot days, when plants may be wilting.

Keep Cuttings Short to Conserve Energy

A cutting's size is also something to consider. I like my cuttings to contain at least two sets of leaves. I use pruning shears to cut the stem from the shrub at about 1 inch below the second leaf node. Since the length between leaf nodes differs from plant to plant, the size of a cutting, using this rule of measurement, will vary. The average cutting should measure between 3 and 5 inches.

To prepare cuttings for rooting, remove the lower set of leaves to open up wounds on the shoot. It is at these wounded sites that rooting will occur. Also wound the end of the shoot's tip by laying the cutting on its side and shaving away a strip or two of bark.

Use Rooting Hormone and Provide Good Drainage

After wounding the cutting, dip the end of the stem into water and then into rooting-hormone powder. Softwood cuttings root more successfully when a rooting hormone is used. The object when dipping cuttings in rooting hormone is to cover the wounds completely. Rooting hormone contains the same auxins already in the stem that initiate root production. Coating the stem with hormone boosts the plant's natural mechanisms to produce roots.

Once a cutting's wounds are coated with rooting hormone, gently tap off any excess and insert the stem into a six-pack or seedling tray filled with a moistened mixture of perlite and soilless mix. This mix provides the good drainage and maximum aeration that new roots need. Cuttings placed into a mix that holds moisture are apt to rot before rooting occurs.

Trim the Leaves and Keep the Plants Moist

Once the cuttings are inserted into the soil, trim the remaining leaves in half to cut down on transpiration loss. These leaves are still performing photosynthesis, even though there are no roots to draw moisture out of the soil. Stick small stakes into the corners of the six-pack, then water the cuttings from the bottom. Finally, tuck the tray into a plastic bag, which will create the humid conditions needed for rooting to take place. Then lace the tray in a sheltered part of the garden that gets dappled sunlight and keep the cuttings moist until roots develop.

Check for Root Development

Some cuttings root faster than others. I've found that the best way to check for root development is with my eyes. After four to five weeks, check the bottom of each tray for small white roots that may be poking out of the drainage holes. If none are visible, another way to check for root development is by gently pulling on a cutting. If it shows some resistance, then it's a good bet that roots have developed. If it pulls out of the tray easily, inspect the stem for very fine root hairs. If no roots are apparent, place the cutting back into the tray, reseal the bag, and wait a few more weeks before checking again. Depending on the species and the growing conditions, a healthy network of primary and secondary roots should develop after six weeks in the bag.

Pot Them up Until Fall

Once they've rooted, pot up the tiny new shrubs into 1-quart pots filled with a mixture of 80 percent soil and 20 percent perlite, water them with a nutrient-rich seaweed- or kelp-based fertilizer, and place them in a sunny spot in the garden. In the fall, unpot them and transfer them to a sheltered nursery bed, where they'll spend the winter. Come spring, you'll have a good supply of shrubs that you can move to a new, more permanent home.

Layer to Make More Shrubs

—LEE REICH

One of the easiest ways to multiply a favorite shrub is through layering: the propagation of woody plants by putting a stem in contact with the soil where the cool, moist, dark environment induces root formation. The technique is simple and has a high rate of success. Because the new plant remains attached to the mother plant until it's well rooted, there's no chance of the top drying out too soon, as can happen with cuttings. In addition, the buds and actively growing leaves release plant hormones that help stimulate root formation. And no greenhouse, mist chamber, or other specialized equipment is needed. Like other methods of asexual propagation, layering produces plants that are genetic replicas of the mother plant. What makes asexual propagation possible is totipotency. Every cell in any plant—except for egg and sperm cells—contains all the genetic information necessary to regenerate a complete organism; under appropriate conditions, a cell can be induced to multiply into roots, shoots, leaves, or flowers. You can count on the plant to do most of the work.

Select the Best Stem

Early spring is the best time to begin the layering process because it takes advantage of a plant's vigor, ensures enough time for the plant to produce an acceptable amount of roots before it is cut away from the mother plant, and provides ample opportunity for the plant to get sufficiently established after it is transplanted.

Pick a Good Spot

Young stems root best and are easily bent to the ground. Once you select a stem, check to make sure that it can be bent to the ground at a suitable location. When I recently layered a spirea (*Spiraea* spp. and cvs., Zones 4–9) in a flower bed, I chose a stem that could be bent down and rooted without disturbing nearby plants. You have no need to restrict yourself to making only one new plant; as many shoots as you can conveniently bend to the ground can become new plants.

If your plant doesn't have any young stems that are well placed, cut back some older stems in late winter to induce new stems to grow. These young stems will be ready for rooting the following spring.

Cut, Bend, and Cover

For some species or varieties, mere contact with dark, cool, moist earth is enough to induce roots to form; other plants require some sort of stem treatment. In these cases, treat the stem by slitting it, then keeping that slit open with a thin wedge of wood; a matchstick, toothpick, or small twig will do. If you are unsure whether your plant requires such treatment, err on the side of caution and wound the stem. You can also apply rooting powders, which are analogs of the natural root-inducing hormones, to the wound area to speed things along.

Set the Stem

Whether or not it requires wounding, the stem needs to make contact with the soil and be held there without movement. Dig a shallow hole and set the part of the stem where rooting is desired into the hole, leaving the free end to come up out of it.

Secure it in Place

Push the soil back into the hole, and keep the stem from springing out of the soil by anchoring the buried portion with a staple of U-shaped wire or a brick or rock. Cover the ground with a thin layer of organic mulch—such as leaf mold, compost, or wood chips—to keep the soil moist and the surface loose so that rainfall penetrates easily. If strictly upright growth is desired in the new plant, stake the free portion of the stem to make it stand straight.

Check for Roots and Replant in Fall

Leave the layered branch undisturbed through the growing season, until autumn. Dig carefully beneath the buried portion of the stem, and lift it to check for root formation. If roots are sparse or lacking, put the stem back in the hole, cover it as before, and leave it in place for another year.

If the stem has a nice ball of roots attached, cut the rooted portion—along with the free end of the stem—from the mother plant. Have a moist piece of cloth ready to wrap the roots to keep them from drying out.

Depending on the size of the plant and the site, the plant can spend its first year in a temporary spot or it can start right off at its permanent home. The latter is warranted if the plant has a good root ball and if the location has moist, well-drained soil.

TIP CUTTINGS

Seven Easy Steps to Tip Cuttings

—STEVE SILK

I take cuttings three times a year: in late spring or early summer, to increase my stock of plants; in late summer, to create plants to overwinter indoors; and in early spring, to grow new plants that will be ready for the garden when temperatures rise.

What You Will Need

Shears or pruners

Single-edge razor

Pencil or pen

Powdered or liquid rooting hormone

Potting medium and pots

Latex gloves (optional)

1. Ready your pots. It's best to grow tip cuttings in a soilless potting mix containing perlite (a volcanic mineral), vermiculite (a micaceous mineral), or sand for good drainage. You can whip up your own mix by combining equal volumes of peat moss and perlite in a 5-gallon bucket, adding water, and stirring. The mix should be moist but not soaked—just wet enough that if you squeeze a handful of medium, a few drops of water dribble out. After the mix is ready, fill your pots (I usually use 3-inch plastic containers).

2. Gently make the cuts. For plants growing outdoors, take tip cuttings in the morning, when the plant's tissues are turgid. To ensure that tissues are well watered, give any candidates for cutting a good dousing the night before. Indoors, tip cuttings can be taken anytime. Use your trusty pruners to lop off stem tips, making sure that each piece has at least three sets of leaves. The stem should not be too woody or too soft; it should snap when bent.

3. Prepare the cuttings. Working in a shady spot, begin by trimming off the bottom pair of leaves right at the stem using a clean razor blade, pruners, or a sharp pair of scissors. Next, snip off the bottom of the stem just below where you removed the leaves. Leave the top two sets of leaves intact, unless they are very large, as with, say, angels' trumpets (*Brugmansia* spp. and cvs.). In this case, cut them in half crosswise so the foliage will lose less water. Finally, dip the lower stem and the wounds where the leaves were removed into a small jar of rooting hormone, tapping any excess hormone on the stem back into the jar. Rooting hormone is reported to be nontoxic, but I like to wear latex gloves when working with any chemical.

4. Pot them up. Use a pencil to make a hole about 1 inch deep at the center of a prefilled pot. Then stick a cutting into the hole, taking care not to brush off the rooting hormone. Don't stick the cutting in too deep, because those that touch the bottom of the container have a tendency to rot. Next, firm up the soil around the cutting so that the plantlet stands tall and there's good contact between the stem and the potting mix. As you pot up the cuttings, transfer them to a tray. When it's full, pour water into the tray to provide a good bottom watering. I let about ¼ inch of excess water remain in the tray. Try to avoid watering from above, since water washing down through the soil carries away much of the rooting hormone.

5. Provide optimum growing conditions. Most cuttings like a moist, enclosed environment safe from extremes of temperature, burning sun, drying winds, and pounding rain. I find that the best place to grow many of my cuttings indoors is in a translucent plastic sweater box placed beneath fluorescent lights hanging an inch or so above the top. I place the cuttings in the inverted lid, with the bottom translucent part placed on top like a greenhouse dome. I slide an inexpensive heating pad—the kind made for seed starting—underneath the box. This setup, however, can be too humid for some kinds of cuttings, encouraging them to rot rather than root. In this case, for better ventilation, I use an old aquarium covered with a sheet of glass kept slightly askew so the setup can breathe a little. Outdoors, in summer, the process is easier. Just put a tray of cuttings in a shady spot.

6. Check for pests and diseases. Check your cuttings every few days to make sure the planting medium is moist and to look for pests. Any aphids or whiteflies should be sprayed with soapy water. Harsher insecticides could harm the fragile cuttings. Also remove any foliage that looks unhealthy or shows signs of fungal growth. If a plant continually sprouts fungal growth or seems to be rotting, it needs better ventilation.

7. Test for roots. Some plants root in a week to 10 days; others may need a few weeks. To check whether a cutting has rooted, tug on it gently. Sturdy resistance means it has roots. If it looks like a plant is not going to root, try a slightly larger cutting with a few more leaves. I've found geraniums, flowering maples, and tropical smokebush (*Euphorbia cotinifolia*) to be among the plants that do best with a slightly larger, leafier cutting. Another strategy for challenging plants is to take a cutting with a heel—a small strip of tissue from the main stem—at its base. Once your cuttings have roots, allow them at least three days of increasing exposure to sun and wind before planting them in your garden.

DIVIDING PERENNIAL PLANTS

Divide When a Plant Looks Good
—JANET MACUNOVITCH

Don't wait until a plant has become decrepit or monstrous to divide it. My rule is that when it looks its best, divide it at the end of that year. Watch for the early signs of trouble: when the center of the plant has smaller leaves, fewer flowers, and weaker-blooming stalks than the outer edges, or when the plant runs out of growing room on its edges and has nowhere to go but into neighboring plants.

Start at the Drip Line
—JANET MACUNOVITCH

To lift a perennial with minimal root damage, begin digging at its drip line. The roots will generally extend that far, so digging there lets you lift the plant with most of its roots intact. Dig a trench around the clump, cleanly severing any roots, then cut at an angle down and under the clump from various points around the outer edge until you can lever the plant out of the hole. For large, heavy plants, you may have to first dig the trench, then slice straight down through the center of the plant as if it were a pie, halving or quartering the clump before undercutting and lifting it.

In early spring, I divide while the new growth is still low to the ground, so the handling of stems is not usually an issue. In summer, I might tie stems together before lifting the plant to avoid damaging them during the digging. In fall, I usually cut plants back before digging them for division.

Know When It's Time to Divide Grasses
—MARY HOCKENBERRY MEYER

1. Divide in early spring, just as grasses begin to grow, because energy resources are still in the roots and buds. Examine plants for fresh growth. Just underground, new shoots may be white or pink. Discard stems or sections without signs of life.

2. Sharpen your shovel, spade, or digging knife. A Hori-Hori knife works well on Japanese forest grass (*Hakonechloa macra* and cvs., Zones 5–9) and blue oat grass (*Helictotrichon sempervirens*, Zones 4–9), but a large miscanthus (*Miscanthus* spp. and cvs., Zones 4–9) requires the leverage of a shovel.

3. Moisten soil to make digging easier. Dry soil is hard to shovel into and makes roots more likely to snap. Soil should be moist but not so wet that it covers a shovel.

4. Remove only a section. You never need to dig up an entire plant, unless you're transplanting it or want lots of divisions. If an older grass sprouts in a doughnut shape, just section off quarters of it. Young grasses, three to six years old, are always easier to divide than older plants. You can sometimes even pull apart young clumps of switchgrass (*Panicum virgatum* and cvs., Zones 5–9) using your hands.

Keep Roots Cool and Moist
—JANET MACUNOVITCH

Fifty percent humidity and 50°F are the ideal conditions for holding divisions until you can get them back into the ground. Put them into a bucket or box in a cool, shaded place, such as a garage, and cover them with newspaper to retard moisture loss. Sprinkle water to dampen the newspaper if the roots seem to be drying during their holding time. If, despite your best efforts, the divisions dry out while on hold, don't despair. Soak them in a bucket of water for about an hour before replanting.

Replenish Soil With Organic Matter
—JANET MACUNOVITCH

If you remove a wheelbarrow full of perennials, then you should put a wheelbarrow full of compost back into that site before replanting to renew the soil, stay ahead of pest problems, and maintain fertility. Without additions, the plants will not have the advantage of renewed, fertile soil and the bed will settle after planting, putting the plants at a disadvantage in terms of drainage and air circulation.

Use Vigorous Sections First
—JANET MACUNOVITCH

After dividing, replant pieces that are, at most, 20 to 25 percent of the original clump. Smaller sections grow more vigorously and tend to produce stronger, longer-lasting blooms. Dividing a hosta, for example, into pieces with about seven growing points will yield the best results. Perennials multiply exponentially—one stem is likely to triple or quadruple itself each year. So if all you do is halve an overgrown clump this year, it will more than double in a season and need dividing again the next year.

Use a Cold Frame

—ADRIANNA VARGO

If you love to use tender or tropical plants in your garden but don't know what to do with them come fall, a cold frame provides a simple solution. It is not a greenhouse: You won't be able to keep your plants growing lushly through the winter months. But you can provide plants with the right conditions for a gentle dormancy, and they will be eager to resume growth come spring.

Whether you are starting seeds in flats or sowing them directly into the soil, a portable cold frame provides the opportunity to get your plants going a few weeks early, and it eliminates the transplanting shock that many plants face because they will be better acclimated from the outset. If you are seeding in the early spring or fall, focus on cool-season plants, as they tend to have lower temperature thresholds for germination. Keep in mind that seedlings are more susceptible to extreme weather conditions than established plants.

Hardening off can be achieved by opening and closing a cold frame over a five- to seven-day period. The key to a trouble-free hardening-off period is to keep track of the extended weather forecast and plan accordingly. If I am moving out cool-season or young perennial plants from my greenhouse, I will wait for a stretch of weather when the lows don't fall below 35°F. Even if the temperature drops after this period, plants hardened off and growing in a cold frame will be fine. For warm-season plants, I wait until the temperatures have stabilized and we are within two to three weeks of our last frost date.

Three types of cold frames

A sunken cold frame with cinder-block walls and a rigid plastic cover is best for overwintering tender plants and hardening off seedlings.

A plastic hoop tunnel warms the soil for spring seeding and protects frost-sensitive plants in spring and fall.

A portable wooden frame with a rigid plastic cover extends the harvest season of cool-season vegetables and allows you to direct-sow seeds earlier in the spring.

Transplant Rose Bushes During Winter Dormancy

—ANDREW SCHULMAN

You'll need to choose a time when the ground is not frozen solid but before the plants break dormancy and begin active spring growth.

Before attempting to move the plants, prune back their top growth to three or four stout, healthy canes, and shorten these to 12 or 18 inches. Dig the roses with as large a root ball as you can manage. Plant them as quickly as possible in their new site, which I recommend preparing beforehand. Be careful while digging and handling the roses that you do not injure their bud union, which is the swollen area near the crown where each rose is grafted to its rootstock.

Set the transplanted roses at the same depth at which they originally grew, and backfill the planting hole halfway with a mixture of soil, organic compost, and a handful of superphosphate. Fill the remaining depression with water and let it drain completely before backfilling to the surrounding soil level. Tamp down the soil gently and water once more. I recommend mulching transplanted roses until warm weather arrives in spring.

Water is essential to transplanting. First fill the hole halfway with soil, then fill it with water and allow it to drain before completely backfilling to the existing soil level.

PERENNIAL HOLE-FILLERS

Everyone has them: gaping, unwanted holes smack-dab in the middle of their plantings. Not long after the promise of spring has sprung, problem areas start rearing their ugly heads. Signs of pests attacking a prized container specimen become evident, your favorite spring ephemerals say sayonara for the rest of the year, and that hot new perennial you planted last fall turns out to be not so hot. But don't let these flops get you down. Failing plants are just a routine part of gardening and an excellent excuse to go shopping. To salvage the season and plug those garden holes, reach for annuals or tender perennials that are long lasting and quick to mature. Here are eight that will carry you into fall with your display barely missing a beat.

—JENNIFER BENNER

'Orange King' coleus

(*Solenostemon scutellarioides* 'Orange King' syn. 'Gold Giant') is a dazzling quick fix in sun or shade.

Zones: 12 to 13

Size: 2 to 3 feet tall and wide

Conditions: Full sun to partial shade; moist, well-drained, fertile soil

'Orange King' coleus is an all-out rock star. With its attention-grabbing copper-gold foliage and burgundy-purple accents, this tender perennial looks great flying solo and yet also makes an exquisite backdrop for nearby cohorts. It is happy in sun or shade, thrives in beds and containers, and asks only for regular water. Like all coleus, 'Orange King' responds well to pruning and pinching, and it propagates easily from cuttings.

'Strawberry Fields' globe amaranth

(*Gomphrena haageana* 'Strawberry Fields') is a thrifty fix.

Zones: Annual

Size: 18 to 24 inches tall and wide

Conditions: Full sun; moderately moist to dry, well-drained, average soil

Although there are purple- and pink-flowering varieties of globe amaranth available, I've found the scarlet 'Strawberry Fields' to be the most vigorous of the bunch. Cheery round flowers (about 1 inch across) top this annual from summer to fall, and its fine stems and foliage provide an excellent contrasting texture beside bold-leaved plants. Globe amaranths are often sold in economical six-packs, which make them easy to pop into places where spring bulbs have gone dormant and left a hole. They also fill in well around young perennials and shrubs that are still puttering along. And as an added bonus, the flowers make great fresh and dried floral arrangements.

Castor bean

(*Ricinus communis* and cvs.) takes plantings for a walk on the wild side.

Zones: Annual

Size: 4 to 8 feet tall and 2 to 4 feet wide

Conditions: Full sun; moist, fertile soil

You want exotic? You got it. Castor bean looks like something straight out of *The Jungle Book*. The towering stems, sporting huge, deeply lobed leaves and funky red seedpods, instantly captivate gardeners. Once the summer heat is on, this plant shoots up like a rocket, filling in the back of borders or serving as a focal point in containers. Castor bean is easy to grow from seed and welcomes an early head start indoors. Just be cautious if small children or pets are around: All parts of this plant are poisonous.

'Prado Red' sunflower

(*Helianthus annuus* 'Prado Red') shines at the back of the border.

Zones: Annual

Size: 4 to 6 feet tall and 1 foot wide

Conditions: Full sun; moist, well-drained, fertile soil

If you've ever seen a field of sunflowers in bloom, the image will live forever in your memory and at least one or two sunflowers will live forever in your garden. These jolly giants scream "Happy summer!" with their huge, traditionally yellow blooms. 'Prado Red' takes this theme and adds a spectacular twist: gorgeous, velvety red flowers as big as dessert plates. These plants are super-easy to grow from seed: Simply sow them directly in the ground in late spring or summer. Use this cultivar to create a lovely screen or to fill in a hole at the back of a border. As the stalks reach for the sun, blooms start appearing about 60 days after sowing.

Flowering tobacco

(*Nicotiana langsdorffii*) mingles well with everything.

Zones: Annual

Size: 3 to 5 feet tall and 2 to 3 feet wide

Conditions: Full sun to partial shade; moist, well-drained, fertile soil

Another delightful annual that is readily available in six-packs, flowering tobacco is a charmer, with 2-inch-long, bell-shaped chartreuse blooms. The gorgeous hue goes well with any other in the color spectrum, making this plant a versatile filler. The flowers keep going through summer and into fall without deadheading and will happily disperse seed to continue the show the following year. If you live in an area with intense summer heat and humidity, use this gem as a filler in spots with partial shade, where it will appreciate relief from the sun.

'Coral Nymph' salvia

(*Salvia coccinea* 'Coral Nymph') packs a flowering punch.

Zones: 9 to 11

Size: 16 to 30 inches tall and wide

Conditions: Full sun to partial shade; moist to dry, well-drained, average soil

Salvias are widely known as flowering machines, and this selection is no exception. Salmon pink flowers shoot from the stems throughout summer and bloom with even more abundance if deadheaded. This garden classic pairs nicely with fine-textured plants, like ornamental grasses, and with bold players, like cannas (*Canna* spp. and cvs., Zones 8–11). Like many other salvias, 'Coral Nymph' appreciates some afternoon shade and attracts hummingbirds in droves.

'Fusion Heat Coral' exotic impatiens

(*Impatiens* 'Balfusheat') adorns bed edges with lots of blooms.

Zones: Annual

Size: 12 to 16 inches tall and wide

Conditions: Partial to full shade; moist, well-drained, fertile soil

This isn't your grandparents' impatiens. 'Fusion Heat Coral' features unique, shell-shaped blooms that impress even the most sophisticated tastes. These flowers seem to pair well with just about any other shade-loving plant. It creates a striking ground cover along bed edges and quickly fills voids in containers. Like other impatiens, this selection thrives in heat and humidity, and it doesn't require deadheading.

'Gingerland' caladium

(*Caladium bicolor* 'Gingerland') makes a splash in shady spots.

Zones: 10 to 11

Size: 12 to 18 inches tall and wide

Conditions: Partial shade; moist, well-drained, fertile soil

Boring is one word you'll never call this fantastic ground cover. Its heart-shaped leaves have a creamy white base veiled in green with coral red splotches and skirted with a soothing green margin. Once warm weather arrives, 'Gingerland' caladium grows like gangbusters, filling in bed edges and vacant spots in containers. Garden centers often sell this beauty potted and ready for planting, but you'll also spot it sold like a bulb—dormant in a bag. Start this dormant tuber indoors so that it will be raring to go by the time it is safe to set tropicals and annuals outside (when nighttime temperatures consistently remain above 50°F).

Give Your Backups a Boost

Here are some additional tips, that will give you an edge when trying to fill garden voids quickly:

- Choose the largest sizes available. To make an impact quickly, splurge for the most mature plants.
- Plant more than one. Have you ever heard the phrase "Two is better than one"? Here's a case where two, three, and sometimes five are better than one. Plant your fillers in generous portions to speed things up. Most tender plants are inexpensive and easy to yank out later if space gets too crowded.

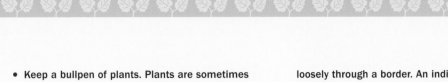

- Keep a bullpen of plants. Plants are sometimes difficult to find after the springtime shopping rush, but that's often when you need them most. Buy your backups at the beginning of the season, and keep them in the wings. Place them in containers on the porch or patio, where they can look great until you need them to spring into action.

- Take out your pruners. Pinching and pruning encourage more growth and make plants bushier. If your new plants are looking a little rangy, don't be shy about pulling out the pruners. Also, keep up on deadheading—it encourages more blooms.

—JENNIFER BENNER

Regional Picks

Northeast

MARDI GRAS SNEEZEWEED
(*Helenium* 'Helbro') sports multicolored flowers.
Zones: 4 to 8
Size: 30 to 40 inches tall and 18 to 24 inches wide
Conditions: Full sun; moist, well-drained soil

European garden designers have long valued sneezeweed for its vibrant flowers and its bloom time, which spans summer and fall. It is, surprisingly, often underused in North America, where it is native. Mardi Gras sneezeweed sports 2-inch-wide, multicolored flowers on rigid stems. The plant has an upright habit that is beautiful in masses or scattered loosely through a border. An individual plant benefits from being positioned in the middle of the border, where it can rely on the support of adjacent plants. I cut sneezeweed back to 1 foot tall in early June to delay the bloom time, encourage branching, and reduce the need for staking.

—ADAM WOODRUFF

South

SPIDERWORT 'SWEET KATE'
(*Tradescantia* × *andersoniana* 'Sweet Kate') is perfect for filling in the gaps.
Zones: 5 to 9
Size: 1 to 2 feet tall and wide
Conditions: Full sun to partial shade; moist, fertile soil

Spiderwort 'Sweet Kate' is a fast-growing perennial that is perfect for filling in those first- and second-year gaps in a newly planted bed or border. From a 1-gallon pot, it will reach its mature size by the end of the first season, and its cobalt blue flowers provide a perfect contrast to its golden yellow foliage. If the plant begins to look tired midseason, simply shear it back to 2 to 3 inches tall (foliage and all), fertilize, and water; within a few weeks' time, it will be lush and flowering again. The plant loves moisture, especially if it's sited in full sun.

—TROY MARDEN

Mardi Gras sneezeweed (*Helenium* 'Helbro')

Spiderwort 'Sweet Kate' (*Tradescantia* × *andersoniana* 'Sweet Kate')

Midwest

BEE BALM

(*Monarda didyma* cvs.) is a hummingbird magnet.
Zones: 4 to 9
Size: 3 to 4 feet tall and 18 to 24 inches wide
Conditions: Full sun to partial shade; moist, well-drained soil

A vibrant red midsummer bloomer, bee balm spreads with vigor—but not as regrettably as its mint cousins (*Mentha* spp. and cvs., Zones 3–9). It makes the perfect filler among sturdy, clumping perennials, like daylily (*Hemerocallis* spp. and cvs., Zones 3–10) and garden phlox (*Phlox paniculata* cvs., Zones 4–8). As summer wanes, don't lop off its faded flowers; the seed heads are lovely in winter. You'll occasionally need to replant bee balm to keep it within bounds, but I've used the heirloom cultivar 'Cambridge Scarlet' as a filler for decades in my garden without complaint, and I also readily recommend the mildew-resistant cultivar 'Jacob Cline' (pictured).

—ALAN BRANHAGEN

Bee balm (*Monarda didyma* 'Jacob Cline')

Southern Plains

WEEPING LANTANA

(*Lantana montevidensis*) can fill a large bare spot in no time.
Zones: 9 to 11
Size: 3 feet tall and 4 feet wide
Conditions: Full sun; moist, well-drained soil

It grows particularly well in containers, too. Weeping lantana provides an understated charm with its purple flowers from midsummer to frost. It is native to South America and has naturalized in parts of the United States, to the point where it has been considered invasive in seven states, though not yet in the Southern Plains.

—LOU ANELLA

Weeping lantana (*Lantana montevidensis*)

Mountain West

SHRUBBY PENSTEMON

(*Penstemon fruticosus*) has bell-shaped blossoms.
Zones: 4 to 9
Size: 16 inches tall and wide
Conditions: Full sun to partial shade; well-drained soil

Shrubby penstemon fills empty garden spots with its many bell-shaped blossoms, which bloom in rosy purple and lavender between May and August and attract bumblebees and hummingbirds. It looks especially nice cascading over rocks. Shrubby penstemon is native to the foothills and cliffs of the West, from Wyoming and Montana to the Cascade Mountains of Washington and Oregon. Trim its branch tips in early spring to maintain a bushy shape.

—TERESA O'CONNOR

Shrubby penstemon (*Penstemon fruticosus*)

Southern California

CHALK LIVE-FOREVER
(*Dudleya pulverulenta*) thrives where other plants fail.
Zones: 8 to 11
Size: 1 foot tall and 22 inches wide
Conditions: Full sun; sandy, well-drained soil

A drought-tolerant California native, this stubborn succulent thrives in rocky soils and on slopes. Its waxy leaves have a striking reflective quality in both sunlight and moonlight. In spring, it shoots up 3-foot-tall flower stalks decked with rosy red buds, making it a favorite among hummingbirds. For best results, plant chalk live-forever at a slight tilt to prevent water from collecting in the crown.

—LAWRENCE ZIESE

Northwest

'GEORGIA BLUE' SPEEDWELL
(*Veronica peduncularis* 'Georgia Blue') is a versatile ground cover with evergreen foliage.
Zones: 6 to 8
Size: 6 inches tall and 1 foot wide
Conditions: Full sun to partial shade; rich, well-drained soil

The foliage has burgundy tints and rich blue flowers from spring to summer. It's a tough plant that attracts butterflies and hummingbirds but, thankfully, not rabbits. In spring, 'Georgia Blue' speedwell combines beautifully with dwarf daffodils (*Narcissus* spp. and cvs., Zones 3–9) while later hiding their decaying foliage. In summer, it can form an attractive mat under larger plants while restricting weed growth with its light-suppressing cushion.

—KAREN CHAPMAN

'Georgia Blue' speedwell (*Veronica peduncularis* 'Georgia Blue')

Chalk live-forever (*Dudleya pulverulenta*)

PART THREE

DESIGNING
your
GARDEN

DESIGN BASICS

TAKE CUES FROM NATURE

Many gardening problems are ultimately caused by trying to force your garden into something that it just can't be. Listen to your plants, your land, and your climate to get some truly inspirational results. Your garden will thank you.

—DONNA OHLAND

Follow What the Landscape Tells You

Focus on the area to be planted. If you follow what the landscape tells you, you discover that the garden is waiting to be revealed. The landscape determines what plants look best, grow best, or grow at all. By choosing only those plants that can handle your conditions, you avoid ones whose poor health makes them susceptible to pests and diseases as well as ones that take a great deal of effort to look good for a short period of time.

Research Your Options Before Choosing Plants

This ensures that selections harmonize with the natural surroundings and will thrive with minimal upkeep. Knowing that you want these qualities helps focus your choices and keeps you from even thinking about plants that just wouldn't contribute to the garden you want. First consider the plant's requirements and tolerance for moisture, wind, soil, climate, and exposure. Rely on native plants.

Let Plants Show You Where They Like to Grow

A natural look takes less work. Letting plants spill over edges and grow in cracks not only lowers your maintenance but also makes hardscape areas softer and more inviting. Encourage self-sowing because it not only creates a more natural pattern to the garden but also teaches you what conditions a plant enjoys or tolerates. In our Texas garden, Zexmenia (*Zexmenia hispida*, Zones 8–10) is one of the most dependable flowers for long-lasting summer color, and its habit of reseeding lends a natural permanence to the garden. Mexican feather grass (*Nasella tenuissima*, Zones 7–11), tall verbena (*Verbena bonariensis*, Zones 7–11), and Dahlberg daisies (*Thymophylla tenuiloba*, annual) have seeded themselves in the natural decomposed granite pathway, making the entryway more inviting.

Observe where plants grow in nature. We've found, for example, yellow columbine (*Aquilegia chrysantha* var. *hinckleyana*, Zones 3–9) growing in the wild under a grand old tree.

Plants Reveal Different Microclimates

You can adjust your design if you notice that a plant reaches into or out of the sun, that something pouts in the heat, or that a plant rots due to poor drainage. As you become more familiar with these microclimates, you can choose plants that are naturally suited to similar situations.

Use a Plant's Personality to Your Advantage

By knowing a plant's natural habit and tendencies, you can place it where those characteristics will have the best effect. Avoid spending time and effort trying to make a plant into something it's not. Let climbers climb and spillers spill. The loose, sprawling personality of winecups, for example, is perfect next to pathways; it spills out to soften edges but is airy enough not to impede passersby.

THREE DESIGN STRATEGIES TO WEAVE YOUR GARDEN TOGETHER

Over the years, I've come up with three helpful strategies to transform collections of individual plants, both on a small and large scale, into harmoniously arranged compositions.

—BARBARA BLOSSOM ASHMUN

Strategy 1: Consistent Use of Geometric Shapes Creates a Sense of Continuity

By taking a shape that already exists in the architecture of your home or landscape and repeating it in your beds and borders, you can create a sense of continuity throughout your garden. For example, if the shape of your patio is rectangular, straight paths would echo the lines of the patio. Square or rectangular garden benches and planter boxes could be used as complements. That is not to say that shapes unrelated to your home or landscape design can't work. They can. Just pick a theme, and use it consistently.

In my garden, most of the beds are oval or circular; their similar outlines create a feeling of familiarity and unity. The rounded beds have curved paths surrounding them in a natural geometry. I've repeated these curved lines and shapes by placing a round picnic table, shaded by an umbrella, and surrounding it with curved benches nearby.

Strategy 2: The Repetition of Waves of Color Draws the Eye from One Area to the Next

I think of a border as a sandwich; the front and back are like bread, and the middle of the border is the filling. If the bread is substantial enough, it will hold a lot of filling. When the edges and backs of your borders are generously filled with waves of the same color, whether from flowers or leaves, you can get away with a lot of variety in the middle of the border and the picture will still look orderly.

In sunny borders, I rely on the yellow blooms of low-growing lady's mantle (*Alchemilla mollis*, Zones 4–7) and the magenta flowers of bloody cranesbill (*Geranium sanguineum*, Zones 4–8) for sweeps of color along the bed's edge. In the middle of the plantings, 'Husker Red' penstemon (*Penstemon digitalis* 'Husker Red', Zones 2–8) stands at attention, displaying clouds of pinkish white blooms atop its maroon stems. Colorful leaves serve the same unifying purpose and last even longer than flowers, usually from early spring through late fall. Shrubs with colorful leaves can be used to line the backs of beds. The best shrubs for this are those that can be pruned each year, which keeps their foliage fresh and their size manageable.

Once your garden matures, it's even easier to pull it together. Look around and select your favorite perennials, such as the ones with good foliage that also bloom for a long time. Divide and distribute them throughout the garden so that they become the links between your beds.

Strategy 3: By Repeating Signature Plants With Bold Forms, You Can Create Visual Continuity Throughout a Garden

You can do this with a series of beds, whether you are working with a large or a small garden space. These can be the same plants or ones that resemble one another, such as perennials with similarly tinted flowers or those with similarly colored leaves. Try repeating leaves with a dissected or grassy form or flower shapes like spikes, disks, or globes. You can also focus on echoing plants with a similar habit like mounded, upright, or arching, which will bring the design together when viewed from a distance.

To tie one long bed together, for example, I repeated clumps of horizontally striped zebra grass (*Miscanthus sinensis* 'Zebrinus', Zones 4–9). These tall beauties look great among late-blooming sedums (*Sedum* spp. and cvs., Zones 3–10), yellow coneflowers (*Rudbeckia* spp. and cvs, Zones 3–9), and Joe Pye weeds (*Eupatorium* spp. and cvs., Zones 3–9), especially when they are backlit by the afternoon sun.

GIVE YOUR GARDEN FOUR-SEASON INTEREST

Four-Season Tips

Large Trees and Shrubs Are Important

Woody plants (evergreen or deciduous) are often called the "bones" of the garden, but this isn't just because they look good in winter when not much else does. Large trees and shrubs provide an ever-present backdrop, so smaller hits of color or texture (from perennials, annuals, and tropicals) are visually magnified. At the back of our pond, we planted a mix of bamboo, deciduous trees, and some evergreens that lend continuity to the view, month after month.

—DENNIS SCHRADER

Add a Few Stars to Pump Up the Color and Texture Interest

Once you have a consistent background, you'll need to pick out a few essential seasonal stars. These are not necessarily plants that shine every day of the year, but they are exceptionally eye-catching—because of their color, texture, or form—during a brief window of time. For our pond bed, we selected a handful of choice plants that steal the show at specific times of the year.

The purple Siberian iris (*Iris* cv., Zones 3–9) in spring, for example, adds a vibrant shot of color that is impossible to ignore. By summer, when the iris has gone out of bloom, the lotus (*Nelumbo* cv., Zones 4–11) shoots up with its smooth, broad leaves. Later on, the lotus adds another element of interest when it bursts into bloom and then boasts interesting seedpods for weeks after. By the time the lotus fades in fall (after the first frost knocks it down), the Japanese maple, with its brilliant coloring, becomes the focal point of this bed. Variegated aralia (*Aralia elata* 'Variegata', Zones 4–9) is another seasonal player that provides interest almost all year, due to its ornate branch structure (highlighted in fall and winter); bold, colorful foliage (which is at its best in spring); and showy summer blooms.

—DENNIS SCHRADER

27 Perennials With Long-Lasting Appeal

PLANTS THAT PROVIDE STRUCTURE

1. Autumn snakeroots (*Actaea simplex* and cvs.; formerly *Cimicifuga simplex*), Z 4–8
2. Culver's root (*Veronicastum virginicum*), Z 3–8
3. Jerusalem sages (*Phlomis* spp. and cvs.), Z 4–10
4. Joe Pye weeds (*Eupatorium purpureum* and *E. maculatum* and cvs.), Z 3–9
5. Meadow rues (*Thalictrum aquilegiifolium* and cvs.), Z 5–9
6. Miss Willmott's ghost (*Eryngium giganteum*), Z 5–8
7. Queen of the prairie (*Filipendula rubra*), Z 3–9
8. Sages (*Salvia nemorosa* and cvs.), Z 5–9 (after a cutback and a second crop of flowers)
9. Sea lavender (*Limonium latifolium*), Z 4–9

PLANTS WITH ATTRACTIVE SEED HEADS

10. Asters (*Aster* spp. and cvs.), Z 4–8
11. Bee balms (*Monarda* spp. and cvs.), Z 4–9
12. Burnets (*Sanguisorba* spp. and cvs.), Z 3–8
13. Coneflowers (*Rudbeckia* spp. and cvs.), Z 3–9
14. Goldenrods (*Solidago* spp. and cvs.), Z 5–9
15. Mountain fleece (*Persicaria amplexicaulis*), Z 5–8
16. Orpines (*Sedum telephium* and cvs.), Z 4–9
17. Purple coneflowers (*Echinacea purpurea* and cvs.), Z 3–9
18. Sneezeweed (*Helenium autumnale*), Z 4–8
19. Yellow wax-bells (*Kirengeshoma palmata*), Z 5–8

PLANTS WITH A DISTINCT WINTER SHAPE

20. Eulalia grasses (*Miscanthus sinensis* cvs.), Z 4–9*
21. Feather grasses (*Stipa* spp. and cvs.), Z 7–10
22. Feather reed grasses (*Calamagrostis* × *acutiflora* and cvs.), Z 5–9
23. Fountain grasses (*Pennisetum alopecuroides* and cvs.), Z 6–9
24. Prairie dropseeds (*Sporobolus heterolepsis*), Z 3–9*
25. Purple moor grasses (*Molinia caerulea* and cvs.), Z 5–9*
26. Switchgrasses (*Panicum virgatum* and cvs.), Z 5–9*
27. Tufted hair grasses (*Deschampsia cespitosa* and cvs.), Z 5–9*

*Denotes a grass that turns a distinctive color in autumn or early winter.

—PIET OUDOLF

12 Ways to Wake Up Your Winter Garden

1. Rely on plants with winter flowers, such as hellebores (*Helleborus*), winter jasmine (*Jasminum nudiflorum*), or witch hazels (*Hamamelis* spp. and cvs.).

2. Feature winter berries like heavenly bamboos (*Nandina domestica* and cvs.), Japanese laurels (*Aucuba japonica* and cvs.), viburnums (*Viburnum* spp. and cvs.), or winterberries (*Ilex verticillata* and cvs.).

3. Include plants with interesting leaves, like Italian arum (*Arum italicum*), skimmias (*Skimmia* spp. and cvs.), and sweet boxes (*Sarcococca* spp. and cvs.).

4. Emphasize plants with intriguing bark, such as crape myrtles (*Lagerstoemia indica* and cvs.), oakleaf hydrangeas (*Hydrangea quercifolia* and cvs.), and paperbark maple (*Acer griseum*).

5. Highlight unusual natural branch structure with Lauder's walking stick (*Corylus avellana* 'Contorta'), Japanese maples (*Acer palmatum* and cvs.), and red-twigged or yellow-twigged dogwoods (*Cornus stolonifera* and cvs.).

6. Attract birds by leaving seed heads of perennials.

7. Prune evergreens into compelling shapes.

8. Invite motion with plants such as grasses.

9. Create a sensory splash with chimes, mirrors, and pinwheels.

10. Showcase large garden ornaments such as planted pots and sculptures.

11. Use interesting hardscape elements like fences, gateways, and trellises.

12. Increase impact with multilevel patios or terraces.

—LESLIE J. WEHR

Watch Out for Wisteria Seedpods

Some seedpods may be left on the vine for winter interest, but just know that if you bring them inside, warm temperatures will cause them to explode. A friend once used the pea-shaped fruit in a winter arrangement. The next morning, she found her cat crouched in the corner, hiding from the flying seeds.

—MEGHAN RAY

Plant Spectacular Spring Bloomers

Early-flowering Options Start the Party Off

Nothing signals the end of a barren winter like the splash of electric blue provided by **'Père David'** **blue corydalis** (*Corydalis flexuosa* 'Père David'). Native to the mountain wilds of western China, this delicate-looking plant has masses of narrow, tubular flowers that are reminiscent of wingless, ethereal blue dragonflies.

Another selection that has multiseason appeal is **mukdenia**, which thrives in rich soil and under the coldest skies without much fuss. Its squat, maple-shaped leaves are a fresh, glossy green. Dense constellations of starry white flowers, however, steal the show. Among a handful of tempting selections is 'Crimson Fans' mukdenia (*Mukdenia rossii* 'Crimson Fans', syn. 'Karasuba').

Rigid spurge (*Euphorbia rigida*) is also an early-spring standout with interesting foliage. This unique-looking plant grows into a knee-high, rounded specimen. It is cloaked with slender, pointed, grayish blue leaves, all neatly set along stiff stems. The somewhat quiet flowers are nestled among much larger chartreuse bracts, for a lasting, electrifying display; this arrangement isn't too far from the festive poinsettia, a family relative.

Although native to northern Africa, **Gibraltar candytuft** (*Iberis gibraltarica*) is hardy enough for a fair number of gardens on this continent. It is a short subshrub with rosettes of wedge-shaped, medium green leaves. Compared to the traditional candytuft, this beefy species offers a decadent flower display. In mid-spring, the whole plant disappears under an abundance of flat, light violet to pinkish white blossoms, creating a lasting mound of color.

Contrary to its better-known vining siblings, **'Flaccidus' spring vetch** (*Lathyrus vernus* 'Flaccidus') is a perennial pea that forms a bushy mound of refined foliage. It is mostly for its early, enduring blossoming that this particular cultivar is sought after. A slow grower, 'Flaccidus' has narrow leaves that create a handsome, feathery look. Small but numerous flowers open pale magenta-pink and gradually fade to a violet-blue.

Dwarf larkspur (*Delphinium tricorne*) is one of those shy creatures native to the woods of eastern and central North America. From its stylishly dissected foliage towers a solid, foot-long raceme of well-spaced flowers. In shades of violet to blue or (rarely) white, each flower is adorned on its back with a long, distinctive curved spur.

—DAVE DEMERS

Late-blooming Selections Keep the Frenzy Going

Graced by large, three-part flowers, **trilliums** are truly an arresting sight. The double-flowered cultivars, consisting of multiple layers of petals, resemble little roses more than trilliums.

California has a wealth of native irises that burst into color as temperatures rise. Breeders have been busy creating garden varieties collectively known as **the Pacific Coast Hybrid irises**; among this lot, pure white 'Canyon Snow' Pacific Coast hybrid iris (*Iris* 'Canyon Snow') stands out.

One of the few plants I've cherished since my late teens is the double-flowered 'Elise Fellmann' snowdrop windflower (*Anemone sylvestris* 'Elise Fellmann'). It produces cream-colored pompons that would put any dandelion to shame. These blooms are marked by the softest touch of green in their center and last much longer than other windflowers.

—DAVE DEMERS

Have an Action Plan for Ephemerals

The rapidity of some spring bloomers to enliven our still-frozen lives is oftentimes matched only by their prompt exit. These disappearing perennials are called "ephemeral" for their short but sweet presence in the garden. As they fall into dormancy, these plants sometimes leave a hole in the all-too-young fabric of our garden. The best way to avoid this eyesore is by planting late-emerging bedmates. The dwarf larkspur, trillium, and corydalis should, therefore, be surrounded by perennials such as hostas, ferns, and ornamental grasses. These companions cover up all traces of our dear ephemerals and protect them from our accidental poking and digging.

—DAVE DEMERS

STANDOUTS BY SEASON

SEASON	SPECIES	ZONES	DETAILS
Spring	'Hawera' daffodil (*Narcissus* 'Hawera')	Zones 3–9	Its fragrant, pale yellow blooms shine in spring. Annuals can be carefully planted on top of the bulbs when they are finished blooming.
Summer	Mexican bush sage (*Salvia leucantha*)	Zones 9–11	The plant's tall stature of soft, gray-green leaves commands attention, and a flash of electric purple blooms in late summer as an added bonus.
	'Heritage' river birch (*Betula nigra* 'Heritage')	Zones 4–9	It has wonderful exfoliating white bark all year and catkin blooms in spring. New, soft green leaves appear in spring and summer before taking on a yellow color in fall.
	Crape myrtle (*Lagerstroemia indica* cvs.)	Zones 7–9	It has great peeling bark, beautiful and delicate new spring growth, outrageous summer flowers, and bright burgundy-red fall leaf color.
Fall	Ornamental kale and cabbage (*Brassica oleracea* cvs.)	Annual	These plants display good foliage color in fall and winter. If the plants survive into spring, they can bolt up and bloom with pale yellow flowers, adding a welcome surprise to the early-spring garden.
	'Miltoniana' copperleaf (*Acalypha wilkesiana* 'Miltoniana')	Zones 10–11	Its colorful foliage looks fantastic from late spring into late fall.

Five Ways to Enhance Your Use of Plant Shapes in the Garden

—MARCO POLO STUFANO

- Sit in a garden and ask: What shapes am I seeing here? Which are dominant?

- Sketch the shapes in your garden, then sketch other possibilities. Or move differently shaped objects around on a table. These exercises can help you get a better feel for how shapes work best together.

- Study artworks, focusing on forms and spaces and how they relate.

- Play with self-sown annuals. Before ripping them out, look at how they play off the shapes of the plants around them.

- Move potted plants around in the garden, observing the different effects that are created as their locations change.

Globes Bring a Bouncy Feel to the Border

—JEANIENE SMITH

I consider any spherical bloom to be a globe. Scattered groups create repetition and rhythm, lending a bouncy, playful feel to the border. My favorites are globe thistles and alliums. Globe thistles provide structure and height, and because alliums keep their shape from bud to seed head, they provide a long season of interest.

Spires Add Elegant Stature

—JEANIENE SMITH

With their stately bearings, spires lend elegance to a border. The best ones are tough and reliable, like the speedwells, Culver's roots, and mulleins. Speedwells come in an array of colors, and some have a bonus of silvery foliage. Culver's roots are like speedwells on steroids; my all-time favorite is the tall white Culver's root. Among the mulleins, dark mullein is the hardiest; it makes a forest of spikes with yellow or white flowers.

Bring Globes and Spires Together

—JEANIENE SMITH

While spires and globes are great individually, repeating these shapes unifies a garden bed. While one spire is an accent—think of a single columnar cedar—several create a theme. The eye takes in the series of similar shapes and passes over the rest of the plants as filler.

Spires and globes also give the garden a more architectural look. They work synergistically, playing off of each other's different shapes to create tension within the bed and between each other. Surprisingly, this theme of two repeating shapes simplifies rather than complicates the border design.

PLANT BY NUMBER

Though most design courses drill into students the dictum of planting in threes and fives, there are ways to successfully incorporate other numbers of plants. Learning how to use each number gives you the tools to forge a well-designed garden.

—JULIE SIEGEL

One Is Not the Loneliest Number

Contrary to its popular musical identity, one is not the loneliest number but rather the ultimate prime number. Unless you have a specimen garden composed of one of everything (a recipe for disaster except under the most skilled eyes and hands), one plant will read as either a specimen or a unifier. If you're going to use a single plant, be sure its qualities are strong enough that it can stand on its own.

Two Signals Formality

Like the guards at Buckingham Palace, the number two conveys formality. Two plants tend to divide your eye, so this number works best when used like sentries to mark both sides of an entrance or passageway. Trees and shrubs are easy to use in pairs, but perennials are more challenging. Some of the larger perennials and ornamental grasses work well in pairs, as do some annuals and tender perennials.

Three Is a Charm

Though three can be tricky in human relationships, this number fits expertly in a landscape. The trick is in the arrangement. Three plants in a row is dull because you know what to expect. If you have enough space, group them in an equilateral triangle. This looks particularly good with mounding or vertical plants. Leave some space between the plants, especially if they are three different kinds.

Four Works Best When Divided

Four can be divided in various ways. Avoid planting two and two, even on the sides of an entry, because it rarely works. It feels off-kilter, always calling for more to make it three and three. A good way to use four plants is by putting one in each quadrant of a circle or square, either planting four distinct specimens or repeating the same plant. Another device that works well is dividing 4 into 3 + 1, positioning three on one side of a path and one on the other. This is especially effective with evergreens.

Five Is Pleasing to the Eye

Five is a number that is used often in designs. A classic example of five is to set up two parallel rows with three in one row and two in the other. This works best in rectangular beds, but it can work in irregularly shaped beds, too. That is not the only way to use five plants. I have found that positioning two plants on one side of a path and three on the other does not work (especially with mounding plants), but having four balanced by a fifth feels right.

Six Is Two Sets of Three

Six works best when it is broken into two groups of three. You can either duplicate the arrangement of threes (in a staggered row or in a triangle) or position them to fill a corner. Dividing plants into groups of two and four doesn't work because it is unbalanced, nor does a line of six specimens, because they will compete for attention.

Seven and More Becomes a Mass

Once you get as high as seven, you have some leeway to either plant in masses or plant the same plant in groups of 3 + 3 + 1. Avoid 3 + 4 because it feels unbalanced. Even numbers higher than seven can be divided into two sets of odd numbers, like 12 divided into sets of 5 and 7. Odd numbers higher than seven can be separated into groups of odd numbers. For example, 3 + 3 + 3 = 9 works, but avoid breaking up an odd number of plants into an odd-numbered group and an even-numbered group such as 5 + 4 = 9. At a certain threshold, roughly around a dozen depending on the type of plant, you don't need to worry about counting anymore.

Leave No Spot Unplanted

—JENNIE HAMMILL

Being an avid gardener with a limited amount of land, I plant every available inch of space—even spots that most gardeners would consider completely inhospitable (like the rocky—but sunny—hill in front of my house). But my hope is to be surrounded and welcomed by plants from the curb, down the side of the house, and all the way to the back garden.

Planting every available inch can start to make your garden feel unruly if you're not careful. But when I first began gardening, I heard a phrase that really struck me. It was something like "Bare soil expresses the poverty of the soul." Heaven forbid. I continue to fill every spot with plants, then go back to edit and space them to achieve a better effect.

Get More Structure and Depth by Using Containers

—JENNIE HAMMILL

Containers add definition to the chaos of many plants. They add a structural element to the plantings and break things up visually. They also provide a splash of color. Designers often tell you to stick to just one pot color in a small space, but this is something I have failed at miserably. I have tried, though, to group my containers somewhat by color or in close proximity to a piece of architecture with a similar hue. Pots also help soften the boundaries of my property. By placing the containers a bit forward, rather than tucked up against the back fence or the sides of the house, I am able to add depth—making the walls seem farther away. This helps me feel like the borders of my lot are disappearing. As a bonus, these containers can also be used to define sight lines, such as placing a pot on a stand at the end of a path—similar to English gardens that use statues on their grand estates but on a scale that works for me.

UNCOMMON, NO-FUSS FAVORITES

The descriptions "rare" and "unusual" are too often synonymous with "delicate" and "fussy"—a warning to any gardener that a plant might take more effort than it's worth. And yet, there are a host of marvelous plants to consider that are underused and undemanding—as long as you choose both the plant and its site wisely.

—MARTY WINGATE

'ELFIN KING' DWARF STRAWBERRY TREE

(*Arbutus unedo* 'Elfin King') is an attractive autumn bloomer.

Zones: 7 to 9

Size: 6 feet tall and wide

Conditions: Full sun to partial shade; neutral to slightly acidic, well-drained soil with medium to lean fertility

Native to the Mediterranean and the southwest coast of Ireland, 'Elfin King' is a pint-size version of the more common 'Compacta', which isn't all that compact at 15 feet tall. Technically a small shrub, dwarf strawberry tree grows well in a large pot or makes a year-round hedge. No clipping or shearing is required when you site it where there's room for it to spread. It's seldom bothered by pests, and it rewards the gardener with autumn flowers while the bright red fruit develops. It's best grown away from sidewalks and driveways, however, because the red fruit—edible but insipid—drops.

MOTTLED-LEAF ELDERBERRY

(*Sambucus nigra* 'Pulverulenta') provides a lot of color from a little bit of sun.

Zones: 5 to 9

Size: 5 to 8 feet tall and wide

Conditions: Full sun to partial shade; moderately fertile, well-drained soil

The mottled foliage of this elderberry brightens partly shaded beds and provides a nice contrast to the shrub's dark-colored summer fruit. In May, pick some of the flat flower clusters to make elderflower cordial, and in summer, use the black berries for jelly. Consider other elderberry cultivars, as well, such as 'Madonna', which has leaves splashed with gold, and 'Laciniata', the green-leaved form of 'Eva' (Black Lace™). Mottled-leaf elderberry is a low-water-use plant when given partial shade and mulch.

'SINGLE APRICOT KOREAN' CHRYSANTHEMUM

(*Chrysanthemum* 'Single Apricot Korean') has plenty of blooms but no deadheading.

Zones: 5 to 9

Size: 2 to 3 feet tall and 3 feet wide

Conditions: Full sun; slightly alkaline, well-drained soil

Always a surprise at the end of the season, 'Single Apricot Korean' chrysanthemum rewards us with fall flowers beginning as late as October in mild regions. The coppery pink petals and golden center blend beautifully with the colors of autumn. Let this late bloomer spill over a sidewalk for a casual look, or prop it up with a sturdy neighbor, like Hint of Gold™ bluebeard (*Caryopteris* × *clandonensis* 'Lisaura', Zones 6–9). The only thing you'll need to remember concerning maintenance is to cut back the plant in late winter. And be aware that new spring growth often doesn't emerge until May.

'SKYRACER' PURPLE MOOR GRASS

(*Molinia caerulea* ssp. *arundinacea* 'Skyracer') provides a perfect vertical, airy accent.

Zones: 5 to 9

Size: 3 feet tall and wide with 8-foot-tall flower stems

Conditions: Full sun to partial shade; neutral to slightly acidic, moist, well-drained soil

In mid- to late summer, the flower stems of 'Skyracer' purple moor grass shoot skyward, providing a surprising vertical element to any bed full of mounding perennials. The clumps of finely textured foliage turn golden in autumn and usually look good until January. The only act of maintenance you need to do all year is to cut the foliage down to the ground in early spring—although if winter weather breaks the plant apart, it's fine to cut it down sooner. Supplemental water is needed only in hot periods when planted in full sun.

EVERGREEN SOLOMON'S SEAL

(*Disporopsis pernyi*) is a slow woodland spreader.

Zones: 6 to 9

Size: 16 inches tall and wide

Conditions: Partial to full shade; moist, humusy, well-drained soil

The arching stems of evergreen Solomon's seal hung with bell-shaped flowers in late spring and glossy leaves all season add a lush note to the woodland garden. It slowly spreads by rhizomes, forming a full clump. Although evergreen, fresh foliage looks best, so cut down all the stems in late winter to make way for new growth. If slugs or snails are a problem in your garden, sprinkle a phosphate-based slug product around the plant.

'GREEN SNAKE' ROSE

(*Rosa 'Green Snake'*) is a carefree blooming ground cover.

Zones: 4 to 10

Size: 6 inches tall and up to 10 feet wide

Conditions: Full sun; moderately fertile, well-drained soil

This ground-hugging rose grows in my parking strip, where it never gets a drop of supplemental water, yet its foliage is always a glossy deep green. 'Green Snake' rose blooms only once—sporting upward-facing, white to shell pink flowers—but provides sprays of tiny red-brown hips for winter. The stems scoot along for 10 feet or more, flat on the ground unless they hit an object, in which case they will hop up and over. Let it intertwine with lavender (*Lavandula* spp. and cvs., Zones 5–9) or hebes (*Hebe* spp. and cvs., Zones 8–11) and around tall low-water-use perennials, such as globe thistle (*Echinops* spp. and cvs., Zones 3–9). Cut back as needed.

VARIEGATED ITALIAN BUCKTHORN

(*Rhamnus alaternus* 'Argenteovariegata') adds unexpected beauty to winter.

Zones: 7 to 9

Size: 15 feet tall and 12 feet wide

Conditions: Full sun to partial shade; moderately fertile, well-drained soil

This is one shrub that requires no shearing or pruning, with the exception of an occasional broken or dead branch. The white margins of its gray-green leaves add a bright note in dim situations, so choose a spot on the shady side for best effect. Variegated

Italian buckthorn's evergreen presence helps fill out the winter garden, and throughout the year it acts as a foil to all-green foliage. For a striking off-season show, surround it with a winter-blooming ground cover, like cyclamen (*Cyclamen coum* and cvs., Zones 5–9).

Regional Picks: Uncommon & Unfussy Plants

Northeast

'MISTY BLUE' BANEBERRY

(*Actaea pachypoda* 'Misty Blue'), a cultivar of a native East Coast perennial, provides three seasons of interest.

Zones: 3 to 8

Size: 2 to 3 feet tall and wide

Conditions: Partial shade; moist, well-drained soil

This new 'Misty Blue' baneberry has beautiful pewter-colored foliage with a slight sheen to it, which lends a soft look to any shady spot. The glaucous clumps are topped in spring with short stalks of fuzzy white flowers followed by white berries in fall. Once it establishes a sizable multistemmed clump, 'Misty Blue' is low maintenance and long-lived.

'Misty Blue' Baneberry (*Actaea pachypoda* 'Misty Blue')

'SUN KING' SPIKENARD

(*Aralia cordata* 'Sun King') is a tropical-looking—yet entirely hardy—plant for your garden.

Zones: 4 to 8

Size: 5 to 6 feet tall and 3 feet wide

Conditions: Partial shade; moist, well-drained soil

'Sun King' spikenard emerges in mid-spring with bright gold leaflets, which can grow to be 3 feet long. It has a shrublike appearance and will eventually form a wide clump. In mid- to late summer, 2-foot-tall spikes of tiny white flowers appear before giving way to purplish black berries. Provide the plant a minimum of two to three hours of sun so that it retains its glowing yellow foliage all summer. As a bonus, 'Sun King' spikenard is also deer resistant and attracts honeybees.

SHREDDED UMBRELLA PLANT

(*Syneilesis aconitifolia*) has—you guessed it—the shape of a cocktail umbrella.

Zones: 4 to 8

Size: Up to 2 feet tall and wide

Conditions: Partial shade; moist, fertile soil

This woodland beauty is a relative of ligularia (*Ligularia* spp. and cvs., Zones 4–8) and native to dry hillsides of the Far East. When it emerges in early spring, the first 4 inches of the plant look like tiny cocktail umbrellas needing a shave, with a fuzzy felt gray over the green. As the plant matures, the umbrella opens and the foliage, changing to a medium green, displays finely dissected leaves with serrated margins.

MERRYBELLS

(*Uvularia grandiflora*) is an exquisite spring wildflower.

Zones: 3 to 7

Size: Up to 30 inches tall and 1 foot wide

Conditions: Partial to full shade; moist, well-drained soil

Related to Solomon's seal (*Polygonatum* spp. and cvs, Zones 3–9), merrybells is native to the central and eastern United States. It naturalizes slowly by rhizomes to form attractive beefy clumps. In mid-spring, the plant displays dainty, bell-shaped, yellow blooms on branching stalks. Because of the weight of the leaves and flowers, the upper portion of each plant nods downward in a merry dangling dance. Plant it under shade trees or along a woodland edge.

—LORI DAVIS

Midwest

WHITE SKUNK CABBAGE

(*Lysichiton camtschatcensis*) is the Asian counterpart to our native skunk cabbage.

Zones: 5 to 9

Size: Up to 3 feet tall and wide

Conditions: Partial to full shade; moist soil

If you plant this perennial in a mucky, boglike environment, it will be happy and long-lived. In early to mid-spring, white skunk cabbage produces large conical green spadices hooded by a white spathe. Soon after blooming, huge rosettes of large leaves are produced. In midsummer, these incredible leaves, unfortunately, must be cut down due to their unsightly appearance.

STACHYURUS

(*Stachyurus praecox*) has elegant vaulting branches.

Zones: 6 to 8

Size: 6 to 10 feet tall and wide

Conditions: Full sun to partial shade; acidic, moist, well-drained soil

Stachyurus is in its full glory for midwestern gardeners in late winter to early spring. It is one of the finest winter-flowering shrubs. Its vaulting branches form stiff arches, and in late winter, the bare stems are covered with 2- to 3-inch-long pendulous racemes of pale yellow flowers. Plant this beauty within sight of your home so that you can be drawn out into the garden to savor its incredible beauty and charm when in flower. I love underplanting stachyurus with hellebores (*Helleborus* spp. and cvs., Zones 4–9).

'ACROCONA' NORWAY SPRUCE

(*Picea abies* 'Acrocona') is on my top 10 list of all-time great conifers.

Zones: 3 to 8

Size: 20 feet tall and wide

Conditions: Full sun to partial shade; well-drained soil

'Acrocona' has a compact, slow-growing, irregularly pendulous form. But spring is when this conifer truly shines. In my garden, it glows like a beacon of light when it produces its showy, immature purple-red cones. A dwarf cultivar of Norway spruce, it will eventually mature to 20 feet in height, but only after 10 to 15 years. Its dark evergreen needles and broad, spreading form make 'Acrocona' Norway spruce an ideal screening or boundary plan.

VARIEGATED ROSE OF SHARON

(*Hibiscus syriacus* 'Purpureus Variegatus') has gorgeous maroon flowers.

Zones: 5 to 9

Size: 4 to 8 feet tall and 4 feet wide

Conditions: Full sun to partial shade; well-drained soil

This variegated wonder is a gorgeous native shrub from India and China. It's not often planted in American gardens, which is truly unbelievable to me because it has such beautiful foliage and is undemanding in its horticultural needs. The maroon flowers are smaller than a typical rose of Sharon. The flower is so unusual that it begs you to stop and examine its intricate beauty. I like to pair this shrub with 'Jungle Beauty' daylily (*Hemerocallis* 'Jungle Beauty', Zones 3–10) because the blossom color is so similar.

—BARBARA WEIRICH

South

INDIAN PINK

(*Spigelia marilandica*) is an easy-to-grow southeastern native wildflower.

Zones: 5 to 9

Size: 2 feet tall and 18 inches wide

Conditions: Partial shade; fertile, well-drained soil

Upright stems are clothed in dark green leaves, and they grow in an attractive clump. The flowers are irresistible to hummingbirds. Though its main flowering is in early summer, Indian pink will often produce sporadic small flower spikes through summer. In a woodland setting, you may see welcome seedlings around the original clump, eventually forming a drift.

STRAWBERRY BEGONIA

(*Saxifraga stolonifera*) is one sweet little plant.

Zones: 6 to 9

Size: 4 to 6 inches tall and wide; 1 foot tall in bloom

Conditions: Partial to full shade; moist, well-drained soil

Allow it to spread along pathways or in the front of beds, where it can be appreciated. Look closely to see the fine silvery veining in the dark green leaves. Like strawberries, this plant produces long, thin runners with small plants at the end. Stalks of small white flowers appear in April or May and hover over the foliage like a flock of tiny doves. Shade is especially important in midsummer heat. Plant strawberry begonia in a spot where the soil stays evenly moist, as it will do poorly in dry locations.

LEOPARD PLANT

(*Farfugium japonicum* and cvs.) has late-summer yellow flowers.

Zones: 7 to 10

Size: 2 to 3 feet tall and wide

Conditions: Partial to full shade; consistently moist, well-drained soil

The large, leathery evergreen leaves of leopard plant are typically shiny. And depending on the cultivar (of which there are many), the leaves might have smooth or richly ruffled edges and might be 4 to 10 inches wide; round to kidney shaped; and plain green, gold spotted, or splashed with white. Its late-summer flowers are yellow, an unusual color in shade-loving plants. On top of its good looks, leopard plant is resilient, well behaved, and prone to few pests. To make sure it stays happy, plant it in a bed generously amended with organic matter and keep the planting well mulched.

Indian pink (*Spigelia marilandica*)

CHINESE GROUND ORCHID

(*Bletilla striata*) has attractive pleated foliage.

Zones: 5 to 8

Size: 12 to 18 inches tall and 1 foot wide

Conditions: Partial to full shade; moist, well-drained soil

We have many beautiful native terrestrial orchids; unfortunately, as a group, they often require exacting growing conditions and can be challenging to grow. But the Chinese ground orchid is not at all fussy and will grow happily in average garden beds. The attractive pleated foliage emerges in early spring. Flowering occurs in April and May, and the flowers are undeniably orchids. The wide, spear-shaped leaves stay good-looking until the plants go dormant in fall, and they provide texture and interest to a summer planting.

—DAN GILL

Southern Plains

DESERT WILLOW

(*Chilopsis linearis* and cvs.) has showers of flowers.

Zones: 8 to 9

Size: 15 to 25 feet tall and wide

Conditions: Full sun; well-drained soil

You can plant this tree singly or plant several to create an unusual hedge. Desert willow has showers of white, pink, purple, or bicolored flowers from mid-spring into fall on a backdrop of soft, willowlike leaves. When allowed to reach its mature height, the twisting trunk becomes a bonus focal point that adds drama. Heat and drought tolerant, this plant also attracts birds and butterflies.

MEXICAN BUCKEYE

(*Ungnadia speciosa*) is a Texas native with outstanding clusters of fragrant pink blossoms and bronze-tinged foliage in early spring.

Zones: 7 to 9

Size: 15 to 30 feet tall and 8 to 12 feet wide

Conditions: Full sun; well-drained soil

The flowers resemble those of redbud (*Cercis* spp. and cvs., Zones 4–10), and they attract butterflies. What follows are unusual trivalved pods with shiny, marble-size black seeds, which are poisonous. Classified as a small multitrunk tree or large shrub,

Desert willow (*Chilopsis linearis*)

Mexican buckeye is revered for its eye-catching fine texture. Its fall and winter interest is equally stunning, with the plant sporting bright golden yellow leaves and grayish brown bark.

BLACKFOOT DAISY

(*Melampodium leucanthum*) has honey-scented flowers.

Zones: 7 to 11

Size: 2 feet tall and wide

Conditions: Full sun to partial shade; well-drained soil

Sun loving with long-lasting flowers, this mounding perennial always commands attention. Blackfoot daisy, with its profusion of white flowers, creates a stunningly beautiful border from early spring until late fall. This plant grows equally well in sun or with a little bit of cover, and it is heat and drought resistant. Blackfoot daisy also happens to be native to the southwestern United States.

TEXAS ROCK ROSE

(*Pavonia lasiopetala*) has velvety foliage.

Zones: 7 to 9

Size: 15 inches tall and wide

Conditions: Full sun; well-drained soil

A heat- and drought-resistant woody perennial, Texas rock rose has velvety, soft green foliage, which sets off delicate yet showy pink flowers. The blooms often last from early spring into late fall. It responds well to regular pruning, maintaining a tighter shape and providing even more blossoms. Known for attracting both butterflies and hummingbirds, Texas rock rose will reseed itself in the garden without becoming a thug.

—RUSS PLOWMAN

Mountain West

'RASPBERRY DELIGHT'® HYBRID BUSH SAGE

(*Salvia* 'Raspberry Delight') is a longtime bloomer.

Zones: 5 to 10

Size: 3 feet tall and wide

Conditions: Full sun to partial shade; average to dry, well-drained soil

'Raspberry Delight' hybrid bush sage has been a stellar performer for me for the past eight years. Few perennials bloom so long and so profusely. Flowers begin in May and can last into early November. Hummingbirds love this plant as much as I do, and it requires little attention. Simply give it an occasional deep soaking during the growing season and cut back dead stems in early spring.

'SNOW FLURRY' HEATH ASTER

(*Symphyotrichum ericoides* 'Snow Flurry') is an especially tough plant.

Zones: 5 to 8

Size: 1 foot tall and 3 feet wide

Conditions: Full sun to partial shade; average to dry soil

It has consistently performed in my garden through some of the hottest, driest summers on record in Denver, thriving on only one or two waterings a month. Forming a textural mound in spring and summer, it heralds autumn by erupting in a froth of white flowers that engulfs the mound for two to three weeks. My only complaint is that I wish it had a longer bloom season. Unlike other asters, I've yet to see this variety self-sow, and it only asks for a yearly haircut in early spring to make room for new growth.

'Raspberry Delight' Hybrid bush sage
(*Salvia* 'Raspberry Delight')

SILVER SPIKE GRASS

(*Stipa calamagrostis*) is interesting from June to March.

Zones: 5 to 10

Size: 3 feet tall and wide

Conditions: Full sun; well-drained soil

A fine alternative to the overused 'Karl Foerster' feather reed grass (*Calamagrostis* × *acutiflora* 'Karl Foerster', Zones 5–9), silver spike grass offers a longer season of interest than most ornamental grasses. Starting in June, this cool-season grass starts to bloom with billowy green spikes that age to tan as temperatures rise. It stays attractive well into March—unless, of course, it's crushed by heavy, wet snows. I have yet to observe any self-sowing on this grass, and it's one of the few ornamental grasses that has actually performed well at the 8,000-foot elevation of my parents' garden.

SILVER SNAPDRAGON

(*Antirrhinum sempervirens*) is a longer-lived mounding relative of the common snapdragon.

Zones: 7 to 10

Size: 1 foot tall and 2 feet wide

Conditions: Full sun to partial shade; average to dry, well-drained soil

The most common snapdragon varieties tend to be annuals or, at best, short-lived perennials. Silver snapdragon blooms mainly in spring and early summer, then again in fall as the weather cools off.

Although most references say that this plant is only hardy to Zone 7, it has performed reliably well for the past four years in Zone 5 at the Denver Botanic Gardens and in my home garden. I find it's especially useful in bright, dry shade. It only needs a bit of cleanup in spring to remove the stems that winter has killed off.

—MIKE KINTGEN

Southwest

WOOLLY BUTTERFLY BUSH

(*Buddleia marrubifolia*) creates a nice contrast when paired with interesting succulents and cacti.

Zones: 9 to 11

Size: Up to 6 feet tall and wide

Conditions: Full sun; well-drained soil

This Chihuahuan Desert native has silver-green evergreen foliage. Woolly butterfly bush will grow up to 6 feet tall but, with pruning, can be kept more compact to fit in small spaces if need be. This butterfly bush does not bloom regularly in the low deserts but does respond to a summer rain with abundant blooming.

Woolly butterfly bush (*Buddleia marrubifolia*)

CANDELILLA

(*Euphorbia antisyphilitica*) is a succulent that works best in partial sun in the low deserts.

Zones: 8 to 11

Size: 2 to 3 feet tall and 3 to 5 feet wide

Conditions: Full sun; well-drained soil

Candelilla is another Chihuahuan Desert native that grows naturally along the Rio Grande. The stems are a pale blue-green color and form a healthy clump, offering a nice contrast to agaves, yuccas, and cacti. Candelilla is resistant to wildlife due to the white milky irritant it emits when damaged.

DESERT MALLOW

(*Sphaeralcea ambigua*) is a spectacular spring bloomer.

Zones: 9 to 11

Size: 2 to 3 feet tall and wide

Conditions: Full sun; well-drained soil

This Sonoran Desert native blooms in many colors, including white, pink, and lavender, but orange is most common. Desert mallow looks best planted in drifts and when combined with strong structural plants, like agaves and yuccas. This plant lives for only a few years but will readily self-seed and pop up throughout the garden. It should not need any regular pruning. Butterflies use this plant as a larval host, and bees are attracted to it, as well.

PARRY'S PENSTEMON

(*Penstemon parryi*) is a Sonoran Desert native and evergreen perennial.

Zones: 8 to 10

Size: Up to 3 feet tall and wide when blooming

Conditions: Full sun to light shade; fertile, well-drained soil

Parry's penstemon creates beautiful rosettes of silver-green foliage with spikes of rosy pink flowers in spring. This plant can be quite showy when a large grouping erupts in spring here at the Desert Botanical Garden. Parry's penstemon is tolerant of many desert climates up to 5,000 feet in elevation. Another benefit is that this plant will readily reseed itself and can become a fixture in your garden for many years, which the hummingbirds will love.

—BRIAN KISSINGER

Northwest

THREE-LEAVED BITTERCRESS

(*Cardamine trifolia*) is a workhorse for dry shade.
Zones: 5 to 8
Size: 4 to 6 inches tall and 12 to 18 inches wide
Conditions: Light to dappled shade; well-drained soil

This thick-leaved woodland gem is one I often recommend for beneath mature trees or established rhododendrons. I completely overlooked watering a small stand during one summer's prolonged drought, and it remained as fresh and as appealing as ever. Patience is required for a season or two as three-leaved bittercress gains ground, but it is well worth the wait.

HIMALAYAN HUCKLEBERRY

(*Vaccinium glaucoalbum*) is a subtle charmer.
Zones: 5 to 7
Size: 2 to 3 feet tall and wide
Conditions: Full sun to partial shade; well-drained soil

Himalayan huckleberry has unusual evergreen foliage that's powder blue on its top side and silver on the reverse. Slow to mature, this compact shrub is a stellar choice in small urban gardens, where thoughtful selection and plant placement really count. As temperatures cool, it shows an even softer side as burgundy highlights grace the leaves and stems. Pendulous clusters of pinkish white flowers in May yield blue-black huckleberries, which birds usually devour quickly.

MAIDEN'S WREATH

(*Francoa sonchifolia*) produces orchidlike flowers.
Zones: 7 to 9
Size: 3 feet tall and 12 to 18 inches wide
Conditions: Full sun to partial shade; moist, well-drained soil

I often forget about this mounding evergreen Chilean native until the lilting sprays of orchidlike pink flowers make their appearance in midsummer and just keep on coming well into fall. The burgundy tones of its autumn foliage are another bonus. If you combine maiden's wreath with the red stems of evergreen huckleberry and the silver-veined foliage of 'Blackthorn Strain' hellebore (*Helleborus* × *sternii* 'Blackthorn Strain', Zones 5–9), you've got yourself a low-maintenance, year-round vignette for partial shade that can't be beat.

Three-leaved bittercress (*Cardamine trifolia*)

HIMALAYAN MAIDENHAIR FERN

(*Adiantum venustum*) is a favorite dwarf evergreen fern.
Zones: 5 to 8
Size: 3 to 6 inches tall and 3 feet wide
Conditions: Dappled to full shade; rich, moist, well-drained soil

You've got to love these black stems. Himalayan maidenhair fern is fantastic as a slow-spreading ground cover in highly visible areas. In 2010, this fern easily weathered a week of temperatures below 20°F and popped back with a vengeance afterward. It is not terribly heat tolerant, however, but occasional water in summer will keep it looking its best. Himalayan maidenhair fern is stunning with black mondo grass (*Ophiopogon planiscapus* 'Nigrescens', Zones 6–11) and variegated London pride (*Saxifraga* × *urbium* 'Variegata', Zones 6–7).

—ALEX LAVILLA

COLOR

&

SHAPE

Move Plants Temporarily Out of Their Comfort Zone

—DANIELLE SHERRY

If you are selecting a sun-loving, red-leaved plant at the nursery, take it to a sunny spot and then to a shadier location to get an idea of what it will look like in late afternoon or evening light. You may be surprised to find that some plants look hot pink in low light, and that may affect your plant selection.

Use Paint Chips for Practice

—FINE GARDENING EDITORS

It can be hard to tell what color shades will work together. Instead of constantly digging up plants and moving them around or guessing about colors at the nursery, head to your local hardware store for some paint chips. They come in every tint and tone imaginable, they're free, and you can mix and match them until you discover exactly what hues you want to combine.

This hot combo relies on broad drifts of plants that are matched in flower color but distinct in texture and shape. Plants, from top to bottom: 'Mohawk' canna (*Canna* 'Mohawk', Zones 8–11); 'Strawberry Fields' globe amaranth (*Gomphrena* 'Strawberry Fields', annual); and 'Smart Look Red' cockscomb (*Celosia plumosa* 'Smart Look Red').

Certain Colors Can Wash Out or Burn Too Brightly

—DANIELLE SHERRY

The classic examples of washed-out colors are white (which can burn your retinas in the sun) and pink (which loses its brilliance in bright spots). Pale yellow is often a better choice for getting "the look" of white in the sun, and magenta washes out to pink in bright light.

··

Use a Color Wheel

—SYDNEY EDDISON

An inexpensive color wheel can guide you in choosing combinations that sing by virtue of their differences or that soothe with calming likeness. Pairing opposites always works, hence the success of combinations like blue and orange, yellow and violet, or red and green.

··

Opposite colors make good companions.

Think Pink for Autumn

—ANDY PULTE

There is no disputing the beauty of fall. Gardens slowly become infused with beautiful shades of red, yellow, and orange, signaling the end of another season. There is a color, however, just one notch over from red on the color wheel, that can be a gardener's best friend in fall: red's rosy relative—pink.

For many, pink evokes a range of emotions. During the height of summer, this unassuming blushlike hue can be overshadowed by the riot of other colors. But later, in fall, pink can become a standout focal point. That's because pink is a color you just don't expect in September, October, or November, so your eye is instantly drawn in its direction. This may seem like an unlikely color to add to the autumnal mix, but it blends in beautifully with traditional fall favorites while giving any vignette a strong visual punch.

Pink can also help tone things down. Because pink is a tint of red (red + white), it blends in with other hot colors (yellow and orange) but takes the level of intensity down a notch. Here are some of my favorite pink plants for fall.

- 'Sheffield Pink' mum (*Chrysanthemum* 'Sheffield Pink')
- 'Pink Frost' small anise tree (*Illicium floridanum* 'Pink Frost')
- 'Welch's Pink' American beautyberry (*Callicarpa americana* 'Welch's Pink')
- 'Neon' sedum (*Sedum spectabile* 'Neon')
- Surprise lily (*Lycoris squamigera*)
- 'Electra' heuchera (*Heuchera* 'Electra')

Indulge In Three Harmonious Hues

—SYDNEY EDDISON

Group colors that share a common pigment and a strong kinship. This trio of colors, which includes violet, blue-violet, and red-violet, would please even Gertrude Jekyll, the discriminating British garden designer who preferred the fine distinctions found in harmony to the invigorating clash of contrast. As a rule, the closer the colors are to each other, the sweeter their song together. For devotees of closely related hues, the frilly leaves of this ornamental cabbage unite blue-violet and red-violet with the deep, true violet flowers of heliotrope, which is about as close to a perfect harmony as you can get.

1. Heliotrope (*Heliotropium arborescens* 'Blue Wonder'), annual
2. Ornamental cabbage (*Brassica oleracea* cvs.), annual

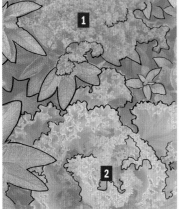

Not All Reds Are Equal
—*FINE GARDENING* EDITORS

If you are trying to create a color echo using red flowers or foliage and it just isn't working, take a close look at the colors. Warm reds (those that contain hints of yellow) don't pair well with cool reds (which contain some blue in them). To solve this problem, look for a pure red hue—and sometimes a pink—to be a partner for one of your plants.

....

Dip into Black Magic
—IVETTE SOLER

Deep, richly colored foliage brings drama to a garden like nothing else, and few flowers have the stop-and-look-at-me impact that black flowers do. Adding a few moody hues to your plant palette is often a slick design move, but there are a few tricks to doing it well.

- Few plants are actually black; most of those we call "black" in the garden are actually shades of deep red, purple, brown, bronze, and midnight blue. Let the entire range of darkness creep into your design. Try 'Red Sensation' cordyline (*Cordyline australis* 'Red Sensation', Zones 10–11), a fountain of reddish black foliage; or black mondo grass (*Ophiopogon planiscapus* 'Nigrescens', Zones 6–11).

- Mix and mingle black plants throughout your beds and borders. If you take a stagger-and-scatter approach to planting you'll have a garden that is bold but subtle, elegant yet playful, and altogether more enticing.

- Stay out of the shadows for two reasons: Plants with deeply colored leaves, like 'Black Scallop' bugleweed (*Ajuga reptans* 'Black Scallop', Zones 3–9), need light to look their best for two reasons: First, most dark leaves lose some of their coloration when planted in shade, giving you a wan, in-between color rather than the richly burnished specimen you were expecting. Second, black plants simply get lost with the absence of light. They're at their finest when creating illusions of depth in a garden's bright spots.

This combo is as high contrast as black and chartreuse, but rather than being cheerful, the gray component creates an elegance. Wormwood (*Artemisia* spp. and cvs., Zones 3–9) is a go-to best friend for many a dark leaf. Here, it mingles with 'Blackie' sweet potato vine (*Ipomoea batatas* 'Blackie', Zone 11) and 'Red Sensation' cordyline.

....

COMBINATIONS THAT WORK

Look Beyond Plants for Colorful Inspiration
—FINE GARDENING EDITORS

When looking for something to spark an idea for a combination, look beyond just flowers, leaves, and stems. Objects such as containers—planted or not—can provide colors to work off of. The same is true of bright ornaments, furniture, or even the trim color of your house.

Build a Leafy Framework to Show Off Bright Colors
—SHARON NYENHUIS

Compared to flowers, foliage has far more staying power. If you select the bulk of your plants for their interesting leaves, as opposed to their beautiful blooms, your garden will look better longer. But a foliage-heavy composition has another benefit, too. Using abundant foliage gives beds a lush, full look and prevents color overload. Hot and cool hues are at their best when used within a leafy green framework. Areas of visually quiet foliage give your eye a break so that when you look at an area with bright color you're more receptive.

Consider the density of the plants you select. Evergreens have a solidity that reads as visual weight. Deciduous trees and shrubs have a light appearance and, therefore, carry less visual weight. To achieve a balance between the two, use more deciduous plants than evergreens.

Movement Heightens the Contrast Between Airy And Dense Plants
—SHARON NYENHUIS

Solid shrubs, such as boxwood (*Buxus* spp. and cvs., Zones 6–9), play off lighter, more delicately textured plants, like grasses, which dip and sway in the breeze while their heavier neighbors remain still. I like to use dense shapes to flank entryways or to mark the end of a garden bed. Because solidity reads as weight, however, place these plants carefully to prevent an unbalanced composition. To offset a long, solid hedge on the left side of a garden, for instance, plant a grouping of equally dense but differently shaped trees to the right. The idea is to have structure for winter (commonly called the "bones" of the garden). Then, contrast these bones with lighter, ephemeral spring and summer plantings.

Combine Soft Tones and Strong Shapes

—SYDNEY EDDISON

Juxtaposing industrial-strength blue and caution-sign yellow creates a sharp, rather harsh contrast because the two hues have no common bond and are at considerable distance from each other on the color wheel. They are just too different. But soften the one to a frosty steel blue and the other to primrose yellow and you have a marriage made in heaven. Set them both against a deep, low-intensity tone of red and you have a plant combination that boasts tonal harmonies enlivened with contrasting shapes.

1. Japanese maple (*Acer palmatum* 'Crimson Queen'), Zones 6–8
2. Globe thistle (*Echinops bannaticus* 'Taplow Blue'), Zones 5–9
3. Nettle-leaved mullein (*Verbascum chaixii*), Zones 5–9

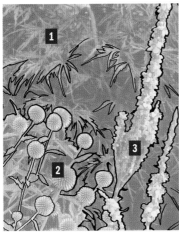

Experiment With Contrasting Shapes and Complementary Colors

—SYDNEY EDDISON

Confining the hues in this planting to yellow and violet (color opposites or complements) gives a degree of harmony to an otherwise highly contrasting combination. While all the colors are either tints or tones of purple and yellow, the opposing forms and textures create tension with the stiff, erect leaves of variegated yucca thrusting out of a mass of smaller, softer, more rounded leaves provided by licorice plant and variegated lantana.

1. Adam's needle (*Yucca filamentosa* 'Bright Edge'), Zones 5–10
2. Tradescantia (*Tradescantia pallida* 'Purple Heart'), Zones 10–11
3. Licorice plant (*Helichrysum petiolare* 'Limelight'), Zones 10–11
4. Lantana (*Lantana camara* 'Samantha'), Zones 10–11

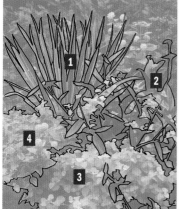

Soften Contrast by Grouping Plants With Similarities

—SHARON NYENHUIS

When arranging plants in a garden, pay as close attention to their commonalities as you do to their differences. A well-designed plant combination takes advantage of both. Select a few specific plants and colors—or, better yet, two pairs of contrasting shapes, colors, or textures—and repeat them throughout your garden. Frequently using purple as a contrast to yellow, for instance, and sword-shaped leaves as a contrast to round-shaped leaves will establish a subtle pattern within your landscape.

Consider Contrasting Leaf Patterns

—SYDNEY EDDISON

Nothing is more restful than a skillfully assembled group of foliage plants. In this combination, created by Wesley Rouse in his Connecticut garden, there are subtle differences in the shades and tints of green. The sooty euphorbia foliage provides a foil for the ice green of the painted fern and also contrasts with the lighter, brighter green of the hydrangea leaves above it. There are also pronounced differences in the leaves' sizes, shapes, and patterns, from the radial arrangement of euphorbia foliage and the elegant, fish-bone design of fern fronds to the large, simple, alternating leaves of the hydrangea.

Red Breaks Up the Green in Light Shade

—INTA KROMBOLZ

Soft colors don't usually work in shade because they aren't dynamic enough to shine in the darkness. Instead, use plants that have blossoms or foliage with vibrant, hot colors. These hues need more sunlight, so areas of light shade are best. Because of their vibrancy, these colors act like beacons, attracting attention not only to themselves but also to their neighbors. Red and most other hot colors are also opposite to green on the color wheel, so they naturally complement the customary hue of the shade garden.

1. Tiger Eyes™ cutleaf staghorn sumac (*Rhus typhina* 'Bailtiger', Zones 4–8)

2. 'Shaina' Japanese maple (*Acer palmatum* 'Shaina', Zones 5–9)

3. 'Gartenmeister Bonstedt' fuchsia (*Fuchsia* 'Gartenmeister Bonstedt', Zones 9–10)

4. 'Alabama Sunset' coleus (*Solenostemon scutellarioides* 'Alabama Sunset', Zone 11)

5. 'Pee Dee Ingot' liriope (*Liriope muscari* 'Pee Dee Ingot', Zones 6–10)

6. 'Filigree Lace' weeping birch (*Betula pendula* 'Filigree Lace', Zones 2–7)

Why it works: Red wakes up other colors. It pairs brilliantly with other hot shades, like orange, yellow, and chartreuse. The best way to maximize the powerful punch of red is to combine it with plants that have similar hot hues but different shapes and textures. The coleus and fuchsia provide the pop of red in this grouping and help draw attention to the lacy texture of the birch tree and the serrated leaves of the sumac. The Japanese maple and the liriope add additional dashes of color.

DAMP SHADE? GET THESE FOUR ELEGANT PLANTS

'Peach Blossom' Astilbe

(*Astilbe* 'Peach Blossom') shines like a fluorescent feather.

Zones: 3 to 8

Size: 24 inches high and 18 inches wide

Damp shade is a must for the fernlike foliage and graceful blooms of this hybrid astilbe, bringing out the best in this popular cultivar. Its lilac-pink blossoms brighten shady spots in mid-spring. Like all other astilbes, the foliage adds interest before and after the bloom period. But be forewarned: If adequate moisture is not provided, the plants will let you know it, as the tips of the leaves will turn brown almost overnight.

Common Bleeding Heart

(*Dicentra spectabilis*) is uncommonly beautiful.

Zones: 3 to 9

Size: Up to 4 feet high and 1½ feet wide

From mid-April to June, 2-foot-long, arching sprays of rose-colored blossoms are set off by grayish-green dissected leaves. It may go dormant by midsummer, producing a hole in the flower bed, but with forethought, companion plantings can fill the gap.

Labrador Violet

(*Viola labradorica* var. *purpurea*) spreads color through the beds.

Zones: 5 to 8

Size: 4 to 8 inches high and 8 to 16 inches wide

Small but tough, this delightful violet flourishes in my damp shade garden, happily popping up here and there to display its small violet-blue flowers 6 inches above its purplish heart-shaped leaves. According to some texts, this plant may not be the true *V. labradorica* but, rather, *V. riviniana* 'Purpurea'. Most important for my coastal Virginia garden, it tolerates heat and humidity.

Lady's Mantle

(*Alchemilla mollis*) performs all season long.

Zones: 4 to 7

Size: 24 inches high and 30 inches wide

Two desirable traits of lady's mantle are that it combines well with other plants and that it has a long season of interest. Light, airy clusters of chartreuse blossoms appear from June through July, but its foliage is its most fascinating feature. The leaves' velvety texture traps drops of morning dew. On frosty mornings, each leaf is rimmed with ice, producing a magical, fairyland appearance. Lady's mantle works well as an edging plant and, left unattended, will self-sow.

—DON BUMA

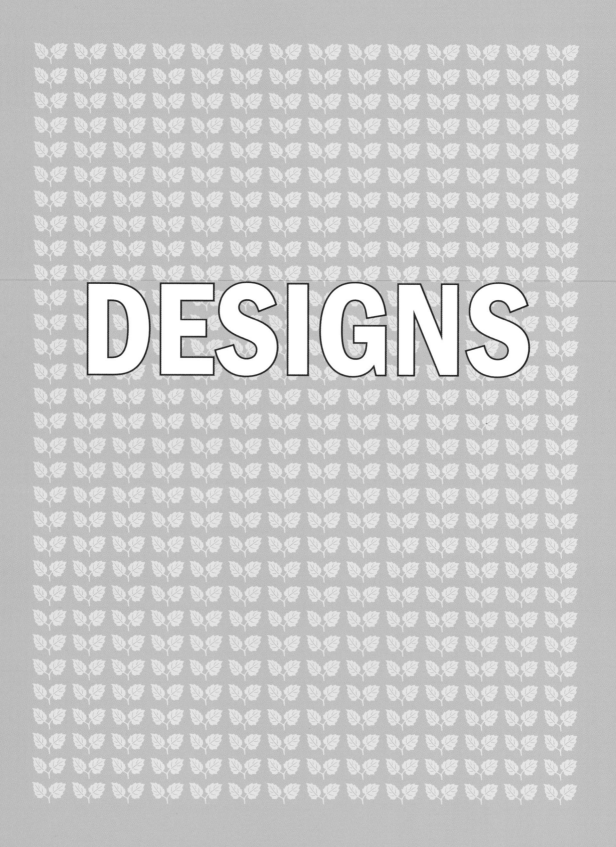

DESIGNS

PLANTS FOR PATHWAYS

Walkable Gardens
—MARTY WINGATE

Garden paths are often edged by ground covers, but why stop there? Adding plants to these normally lifeless voids can soften the look of brick and stepping-stone paths while providing a natural weed and erosion suppressant.

To choose the right plants for paths, consider each plant's foot-traffic tolerance. Some ground covers don't mind being stepped on, while others resent it. It's important to go for plants that meet your path's light, water, and soil requirements as well as its traffic level.

Favorites for Occasional Footfalls

Plant 'Blue Haze' acaena (*Acaena* 'Blue Haze', syn. *A.* 'Pewter', Zones 7–9) in areas of your garden that you visit seasonally. It does not like to be stepped on often, so place it where you need to do only periodic weeding. 'Kewensis' wintercreeper (*Euonymus fortunei* 'Kewensis', Zones 5–9) has wonderful tiny leaves that add a nice texture underfoot. It grows in a mounding form but has a remarkable way of shooting upward if it encounters a vertical surface. Sometimes plants underfoot are volunteers. Beach strawberry has happily migrated to a mulched path in the author's garden, where its glossy evergreen leaves and red stems are a vision of perfection.

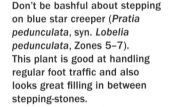

Don't be bashful about stepping on blue star creeper (*Pratia pedunculata*, syn. *Lobelia pedunculata*, Zones 5–7). This plant is good at handling regular foot traffic and also looks great filling in between stepping-stones.

Favorites for Steady Traffic

Brass buttons (*Leptinella squalida* and cvs., syn. *Cotula squalida*, Zones 4–7) is an excellent ground cover that requires minimal weeding. Plants will form a tight carpet of green in just a year.

Woolly thyme (*Thymus pseudolanuginosus*, Zones 5–9) likes to stretch its flat branches out over sidewalks and stairs. It is useful in softening the lines created by hardscaping materials like brick and concrete.

CREATE A HEALING GARDEN

Healing gardens of the past were often located in sacred places like cloistered gardens within monasteries and Zen gardens surrounding Buddhist temples. They served as contemplative places to restore the mind, body, and spirit. Today, healing gardens are often designed for public spaces to alleviate the stresses of daily life. They are commonly found at corporate campuses, to help employees relax, and on the grounds of hospitals and hospices to provide comfort. We can create healing gardens in our own private spaces, as well.

Fragrance is a key to healing for many gardeners. The scents of rosemary, roses, lilies, and honeysuckle evoke feelings of joy that heal the sorrows of the day.

Color, too, can lift the spirit. For many, white is the most uplifting color, perhaps because it reminds us of light and purity. Pastels are comforting: Pale 'Visions in Pink' astilbe, baby blue 'Summer Skies' delphinium, and creamy yellow 'Anthea' yarrow are tranquilizing and easy on the eyes. Some gardeners need a shot of heat to heal.

Water is also important to a healing garden. The reflective surface of still water can help a busy mind quiet down. Water attracts birds and butterflies, adding another pleasurable dimension to the garden. Use a pond or even a simple water bowl to achieve this. In my own garden, I rely on several birdbaths.

The sounds of a bubbler, creek, or waterfall have a cleansing effect. Other sounds evoke restfulness: the rustling of ornamental grasses or the ring of a gong, reminiscent of a temple bell's call.

Japanese garden style, with its meticulously pruned plants, is a good model for a healing garden. The strong sense of order is calming to the mind, and the predominance of green foliage sets a quiet mood. Places to sit and gaze are important, too, especially in the comforting, dappled light beneath the tree canopy. Sculpture, such as icons of serenity like Buddha and St. Francis, can soothe and heal by reminding us of love and compassion.

—BARBARA BLOSSOM ASHMUN

COLD-CLIMATE GARDENING

There are a number of plants that are troopers no matter how harsh the winter or spring. As a general rule, those that die back to the ground each fall do better than evergreen perennials.

—AMY HINMAN

Grow Hardy Perennials

In my Montana garden, the perennial cornflower (*Centaurea montana*) often blooms by the beginning of May. After it flowers, I cut it back by two-thirds and it blooms again by the end of summer. Another early riser is oregano (*Origanum vulgare*). Artemisias (*Artemisia ludoviciana* 'Silver King' and 'Silver Queen') poke through the soil much later but are consistent every year, along with other herbs like valerian (*Valeriana officinalis*), bee balm (*Monarda didyma*), and anise hyssop (*Agastache foeniculum*). These tough plants will continue blooming through an unexpected midsummer frost.

Domesticated varieties of wildflowers also do well. Lupines (*Lupinus* cvs.) are early-summer bloomers that generously reseed themselves. *Delphinium* cultivars—6-foot giants compared to their cousin, the native larkspur—love the cool temperatures and pull through most winters without a problem.

Peonies (*Paeonia* cvs.), bearded irises (*Iris* cvs.), sneezewort (*Achillea ptarmica* 'The Pearl'), sea holly (*Eryngium maritimum*), and tansy (*Tanacetum vulgare*) are also sound choices for tough climates.

Stagger the Seedlings in Patterns

—JENNIFER BARTLEY

Instead of lining up crops in perfect rows, stagger the seedlings in a triangular pattern so that the bed fills in with a mass of color.

Create an edible oasis. Raised beds, pathways, color blocks, and boundary plantings transform your veggie plot into a beautiful kitchen garden.

Arrange bunches of bold color. Vibrant, lush foliage defines a kitchen garden. Plant colorful sections of flowers, vegetables, fruits, and herbs next to one another to achieve a truly dramatic display.

Define your space. Fences, walls, and living borders help frame your garden. Establish a peaceful outdoor retreat by choosing options that best fit your style.

Plant snug beds. Rather than planting everything in straight rows separated by expanses of soil, consider creating tight planting patterns that will provide an expanse of attractive edibles.

Smooth out the edges. Clean edges and pathways help define your space. You can also unify garden and home by employing complementary colors and materials (wood and brick, for example).

Easy, Long-Lasting Kitchen-Garden Favorites

—JENNIFER BARTLEY

- Nasturtiums (*Tropaeolum* spp. and cvs.). These easy-to-grow edible annuals make great edging plants. The flower colors vary from scarlet red and orange to creamy white.

- 'Tangerine Gem' marigold (*Tagetes tenufolia* 'Tangerine Gem'). This plant's tiny, edible orange flowers have a citruslike fragrance and appear all season. The foliage is delicate and feathery, mounding to about 8 inches tall.

- Italian parsley (*Petroselinum crispum* 'Italian Plain Leaf'). This flat-leaf parsley stays a rich green all summer. A flavorful variety, it can be used daily in the kitchen. It tolerates some shade.

- Red mustard (*Brassica juncea* 'Osaka Purple'). The fast-growing large leaves are red on one side and green underneath. Their spicy flavor makes them great for sandwiches and salads. Sow it in early spring directly in the garden.

- Scarlet runner bean (*Phaseolus coccineus*). This gorgeous climber covers trellises with striking, edible red flowers, tasty beans, and leafy green vines. It's an heirloom variety that also attracts hummingbirds.

- Artichoke (*Cynara scolymus*). The massive, spiny leaves of artichoke take up a lot of space but fill a planting with gusto. Once the flower bud comes into season, it makes a wonderful starter for any meal.

- Lettuces (*Lactuca sativa* and cvs.). These amazing plants come in a variety of colors and shapes. The leaves can be cut-and-come-again or allowed to swell into round balls.

PART FOUR

MAINTAIN, PRUNE, WEED & HARVEST

GENERAL MAINTENANCE

Whip Your Garden Into Shape

—TRAVIS RUMSEY

Need to spruce up your garden in a hurry (for a party or guests)? Follow the ACE approach:

A = Assess the Garden
- Determine where people will gather.
- Find the most noticeable problems.
- Identify areas with seasonal interest.

C = Clean Up Problems
- Remove unhealthy plants and plant parts: dead plants, dead branches, dead leaves, weeds, and spent flowers.
- Create crisp lines by mowing, trimming, and edging the lawn.
- Clean all hardscaping. Sweep or power-wash patios, paths, or fountains as needed and as time allows.

E = Enhance What You Have
- Capture your guests' attention with an eye-catching table and a beautiful patio stage.
- Add color for interest. Install blooming or bright-foliage plants where they will make a difference, either in colorful pots or to fill gaps in beds.
- Design an inviting entry. Include elements from your garden to hint at what guests will experience inside.
- Add fresh mulch. A thin layer, just enough to cover the old mulch or to cover any bare patches, will do wonders.

Forgo Finesse During Fall Cleanup

—KERRY A. MENDEZ

By mid-autumn, the joy of gardening has usually worn thin and I'm ready to mow down the whole kit and caboodle. Depending on my mood, I will use a lawn mower, weed whacker, miniature chain saw, or hedge trimmer to whack almost everything in my perennial garden to within a few inches of the ground. Don't worry. The plants can take it, and it's a great release after a rough day with the kids, at the office, or in traffic.

Anytime after October 1 is the best time to have at it in my Zone 4 yard. Be sure to rake sheared foliage from your beds to reduce future fungal and insect problems. Skip over woody-based plants, like lavenders (*Lavandula* spp. and cvs., Zones 5–9). They resent being pruned in the fall. You may also want to bypass plants like purple coneflowers and ornamental grasses for winter interest or to feed the birds.

TOOL MAINTENANCE

Clean, sharp tools work better. Following a regular maintenance routine also means fewer blisters and backaches.

—KEN TEXTOR

Clean Tools Last Longer

After every use of tools that you use to work the soil, wash soil and grime from them with a steady spray of water from the garden hose. Doing so keeps diseases, fungi, insect eggs, and weed seeds from being unwittingly spread around the garden. Cleaning also extends the life of a tool by removing moisture-laden, rust-enhancing soil from steel surfaces.

After washing any tool, dry it with a cotton rag before putting it away. Tools that don't come in contact with soil, particularly those with sharpened edges like axes, pruning shears, and knives, should be wiped down with a thick, rough cotton cloth to remove any gums and saps from their blades. When working on pitch-producing plants like conifers, dampen the cloth with a little paint thinner before wiping. In all cases, once dirt and residue are removed, dry the tool with a clean cotton rag.

Apply Oil to Prevent Rust

Oil steel tool heads to prevent them from oxidizing. The oil creates a barrier between the air and the steel. When applied to steel surfaces, the oil insulates the steel and prevents it from oxidizing. To thin the oil out and make it easier to work with and to better coat both porous and smooth steel surfaces, I mix 1 quart of non-detergent 30W motor oil (any brand will do) with a pint of kerosene or lamp oil. This 2:1 ratio of oil to kerosene can either then be wiped onto the steel surface with a clean cotton rag or sprayed on to metal surfaces—a recycled household-cleaner spray bottle works for me. Store the mixture away from heat sources and dispose of it as you would any motor oil.

Whichever way the oil is applied, keep the coating thin so it won't drip off the tool head and onto the floor. Because oil is organically based and breaks down rapidly in soil, you don't have to worry about this small amount of oil adversely affecting your soils.

Remove Rust With a Wire Brush

Extremely rusty tools require special attention. I use a sheet of 80-grit sandpaper to remove light coatings of rust. For a slightly heavier coat, a stiff wire brush can be effective. But when rust has turned a steel surface rough, like the texture of medium-grit sandpaper, a heavy-handed approach is needed. On badly pitted steel surfaces like those on tools you find at yard sales, the quickest and most sensible option is an electric drill with a wire-brush attachment. Always wear safety glasses to protect your eyes. Once I've removed as much rust as possible, I then apply a coat of my oil mixture to the newly exposed steel to stop the oxidation process in its tracks and keep in check the almost invisible residual rust that I couldn't remove.

Sharpen Tools for Peak Efficiency

Some tools like shovels, axes, hoes, and trowels are best sharpened with a hand file, while other tools like pruning shears and knives call for a honing stone. Depending on how dull an edge is, some tools may require a session with a high-speed grinding stone.

- Use a hand mill file to sharpen hoes and shovels. The key to successful sharpening is keeping the tool steady and the file at the proper angle.

- Sharpen pruning blades and knives by sliding an oiled honing stone in one direction across the tool's beveled edge.

- Grind battered tools into shape. Lawnmower blades and axes that take a lot of abuse deserve an annual trip to a grinder.

PLANTS THAT CAN WEATHER WINTER'S WORST

When you live in a cold climate, winter can wreak havoc on your plants. During cold, dry, windy winters, perennials can die by spring from desiccation, while during cold, wet, snowy winters, perennials often rot at the roots. We asked experts from two different extreme climates—Dan Johnson in Denver and Scott Endres in Minneapolis—to recommend perennials that can take anything their tough winters throw at them and come back even stronger, spring after spring.

Plants That Can Take Cold and Dry

In the West, wide-open spaces, blue skies, and low humidity present challenges for those inclined to garden. Low humidity desiccates plants that have thin bark or delicate leaves. Intense sunlight may burn plants that would like full sun elsewhere. You might imagine that these tribulations are restricted to summer, but winter often intensifies the challenge. Dry, cold winds can freeze-dry plants to their core, which is especially stressful for broadleaf evergreens and plants with thin bark. Dry air and winter sunshine create wide temperature swings of up to 40°F, with 50°F days followed by bitterly cold nights in the teens. Repeated freezing and thawing can dry out soil and heave new plants out of the ground.

The steppes and high deserts of the West demand specially adapted plants, whether native or from similar climates elsewhere. Choosing the best plants can help you beat the odds and makes for dazzling, uniquely western summer gardens.

Mexican hat (*Ratibida columnifera* and cvs.) has a cheerful demeanor.

Clear gold-reflexed petals dance around a central cone like a hula skirt. The flowers

Mexican hat (*Ratibida columnifera* and cvs.)

stand neatly above the foliage like a dance troupe poised to perform. This tough-as-nails gem thrives on neglect and reseeds easily into open ground. Its basal rosettes of foliage are evergreen, and the dried seed heads persist into winter.

Amethyst sea holly (*Eryngium amethystinum*) is one of the best of the sea hollies.

A comfortable border-size plant, it stays where you put it and never fails to elicit inquiries. Deep roots make it tough and care-free. Sharply toothed leaves give a preview of the spine-tipped flowers that appear in midsummer. The starry bracts that surround the flowers appear to be snipped carefully out of iridescent sheets of painted metal. The effect is long lasting, and the flowers may be cut and dried or left to stand into winter.

Amethyst sea holly (*Eryngium amethystinum*)

Butterfly weed (*Asclepias tuberosa* and cvs.) warms up the border with glowing flowers.

This milkweed does not spread underground like some of its genus, and it's one of the few milkless members of the milkweed family. A deep taproot ensures drought tolerance once established. The flowers are irresistible to butterflies and other native pollinators. Butterfly weed is spectacular when paired with other prairie inhabitants, like Mexican hat and blue grama grass (*Bouteloua gracilis*, Zones 5–9).

'Silver Blade' evening primrose (*Oenothera macrocarpa* ssp. *incana* 'Silver Blade') is a plant for every garden.

It's resilient if abused and thrives even in unwatered gardens once established. Everything about this plant has a luminous quality, from its broad silvery leaves to its 3-inch-wide, lemony yellow flowers. It blooms from late spring into fall, continuing even after the first frost of the season. It performs as a lax ground cover, or you can show it off cascading over retaining walls or boulders. Deep, tuberous roots ensure survival through heat, drought, and cold.

Golden columbine blooms long and reliably.

The blue columbine (*Aquilegia caerulea*, Zones 3–8) of the Colorado high country may have more notoriety, but its cousin, golden columbine, will bloom longer in most gardens. Found naturally in low canyons and vertical sandstone seeps, this cheerful wildflower thrives in the average sunny garden or in bright, dry shade with occasional water. Deadheading prolongs the display, but allow the last seed capsules to ripen, as the plant will reseed itself where conditions suit it.

Dotted blazing star is super hardy.

The most common blazing star available—even in the West—is the eastern species, *Liatris spicata* (Zones 4–9), found in moist, sunny meadows within its range. But its shallow roots are poorly adapted to the drier conditions of the West. Luckily, we have one of our own. Dotted blazing star (*Liatris punctata*) survives with a deep taproot that sails through even our worst droughts and takes winter cold in stride. Its compact habit stands up to wind and even most hail.

Harriman's yucca (*Yucca harrimaniae*) is an artful addition.

Any yucca will add a quintessential western feel to a garden. Experimentation is a worthy endeavor, as even some of the tree-type species can prove hardy in the right microclimate. But for reliable success and manageable proportions, Harriman's yucca is a safe and rewarding bet. Its leaves are stiff and narrow, with curling white threads along their edges. Sometimes referred to as the "dollhouse yucca," selected forms of Harriman's yucca may have rosettes as small as 6 inches across, accenting a dry border or rock garden like small works of fine art. Good drainage, winter dryness, and full sun are essential. Rhizomatous roots may slowly increase its spread and ensure its survival.

Plants That Can Take Cold and Wet

In the upper Midwest, the extremely cold winters and heavy snowfalls can be brutal, but ironically, the cold and the snow are the good guys. If doled out gradually, the cold sends our hardy plants into a deep, restful dormancy. Normal snowfalls provide a layer of insulation that stabilizes soil temperatures, protecting the sleeping beauties underneath. In theory, plants emerge in spring better than ever after their long nap. Trouble arises when Jack Frost doesn't get the recipe just right. Drastic changes in air temperature make for less-than-ideal thaw-and-freeze cycles, causing ice pack at the soil surface and rotting the plants below. The same extreme temperature swings during dry winters without snow cover can cause huge temperature fluctuations in surface soil, resulting in plants going in and out of dormancy. A layer of mulch applied after the soil temperatures drop at or near freezing may minimize the threat of winter casualties, but it's not guaranteed. Certain perennials will grow no matter what winter brings. Here are a few of my favorite perennials that never fail to impress with their endurance and good looks.

Dwarf Solomon's seal (*Polygonatum humile*) has cute pudgy green stems.

Underused but always appreciated, dwarf Solomon's seal offers an alternative to the handful of shade-tolerant ground covers northern gardeners have in their back pocket. Those cute stems and horizontally stacked leaves form tight colonies even in dry shade. And just when you think things can't get any better, the plant also boasts delicate, bell-shaped white flowers in mid-spring. Because of its extreme hardiness, expect dwarf Solomon's seal to become a fixture in your shade garden.

Dwarf Solomon's seal (*Polygonatum humile*)

The gas plant (*Dictamnus albus*) is surprisingly attractive.

Don't let the name fool you—this hardy perennial with the not-so-flattering name has sexy good looks when in flower and handsome seedpods and foliage the rest of the season. Never needing dividing or staking, this workhorse perennial gets better each year. It's a bit slow to establish itself but will make up for lost time with decades of blooming.

Dwarf goatsbeard (*Aruncus aethusifolius*) loves the shade.

When I am looking for a tough shade plant that is not a hosta, I will often migrate toward goatsbeard (*Aruncus* spp. and cvs., Zones 3–9). Dwarf goatsbeard (*Aruncus aethusifolius*), one my favorites, boasts fine-textured, fernlike foliage and creamy white astilbe-resembling flowers. This hardy soul will stand up to the harshest winters without batting an eye. Always reliable, always beautiful, and a complement to almost anything you pair it with, dwarf goatsbeard makes an impact that is never less than impressive.

'Hot Lips' turtlehead (*Chelone lyonii* 'Hot Lips') heats up the fall.

When everything else has finished blooming in the perennial border, 'Hot Lips' turtlehead picks up where others have left off. A late bloomer, the clear pink flowers are always a welcome addition to the notoriously green and bloomed-out garden of late summer and fall. 'Hot Lips' boasts glossier leaves than other turtleheads, adding to its star quality. 'Hot Lips' will spread into a noninvasive colony each year, and it easily transplants to other parts of the garden.

Ground clematis (*Clematis recta* and cvs.) has lovely foliage and blooms.

It seems like the hardiest plants always have the most unappealing names. Ground clematis (*Clematis recta* and cvs.) fits right in, but this Cinderella story is so lovely in the garden. This bush-type clematis is content to live out its days supported by a peony hoop or, better yet, happy to be given the freedom to billow out over a garden wall. Purple-tinged foliage and interesting seed heads make ground clematis attractive well after the clouds of pure white flowers have disappeared.

Cushion spurge (*Euphorbia polychroma* and cvs.) earns its keep all season long with cheerful yellow blooms emerging in spring above fine-textured foliage.

Its good looks continue into fall with an excellent reddish fall-foliage color. Cushion spurge loves the hot sun and, once established, will even tolerate dry, poor soils. Clumps are not aggressive and are wonderful as single specimens in small gardens or in larger groups, if space allows.

'Biokovo' hardy geranium (*Geranium × cantabrigiense* 'Biokovo') will endure just about whatever you throw at it.

This super-hardy geranium can take sun, shade, and dry shade with ease. Unlike many perennial geranium varieties, 'Biokovo' is never floppy. Pink flower buds open to blush-colored flowers in spring. The foliage is attractive throughout the season and turns a pleasing orange-red in fall. This excellent ground cover is bulletproof in every respect.

Regional Picks

Northeast

AUTUMN RADIANCE® MAPLE

(*Acer rubrum* 'Autumn Radiance') is not just another red maple.

Zones: 4 to 7

Size: Up to 30 to 50 feet tall and wide

Conditions: Full sun to partial shade; moist, well-drained soil

This may look like just another boring red maple, but it's not. Autumn Radiance colors up in fall about two weeks earlier than most other maples and really glows in the sunlight. Its strong, uniform limbs help it ward off threats of breakage under heavy snow, which makes it ideal for the Northeast. The silvery gray bark is an added bonus, while its broad oval canopy creates a nice shady place to hide under in the heat of summer.

'POWDER GIANT BLUE' WOODLAND IRIS

(*Iris cristata* 'Powder Giant Blue') is a spreading beauty.

Zones: 3 to 9

Size: 6 to 8 inches tall and wide

Conditions: Partial to full shade; moist, well-drained soil

'Powder Giant Blue' woodland iris has great straplike blue-green foliage and dainty purple flowers in mid-spring. I received this plant as a gift many years ago, and since then, I've run it over with a lawn mower, sprayed it with Roundup®, and even forgotten to find it a new home when we moved (I literally just threw it under our deck and hoped for the best); despite all this, it's still thriving. The plant has always pulled through winter well, surviving under heavy snow laced with road salt.

JAPANESE TREE LILAC

(*Syringa reticulata*) stands up to tough conditions beautifully.

Zones: 3 to 8

Size: 20 to 30 feet tall and 15 to 20 feet wide

Conditions: Full sun to partial shade; moist, well-drained soil

For years, I have marveled at some Japanese tree lilacs along the Connecticut shore, which seem to thrive despite being subjected to high winds, salt spray, road salt, heavy snow loads, and kids hanging monkeylike on their lower limbs. This stand of trees never skips a beat. With a fairly upright habit, this plant would fit into almost any setting without taking up a large amount of space.

'UNIQUE' PANICLE HYDRANGEA

(*Hydrangea paniculata* 'Unique') is tough, with a delicate fragrance.

Zones: 4 to 8

Size: 10 to 15 feet tall and 8 feet wide

Conditions: Full sun to partial shade; well-drained soil

When a plant thrives in Maine, you know that it's tough. While visiting that state years ago, I was surprised to discover that the flowers of this shrub have a subtle scent—the only fragrant hydrangea I know of. 'Unique' panicle hydrangea also has sturdy branches that help it persevere against strong winter winds and the heaviest snow loads. I like to cut this plant back in late fall and then thin some branches in early spring to get the biggest and best blooms.

—ED GREGAN

Mid-Atlantic

'BRILLIANCE' AUTUMN FERN

(*Dryopteris erythrosora* 'Brilliance') is carefree and colorful.

Zones: 5 to 9

Size: 22 inches tall and 18 inches wide

Conditions: Partial to full shade; moist, rich, well-drained soil

'Brilliance' is an improved form of autumn fern. Still semi-evergreen, with great texture and even more color, 'Brilliance' offers bright copper new growth in spring that turns green in summer and russet in fall. This tough fern reliably rebounds from snow cover and stands up to cold winds. Once established, 'Brilliance' requires little care, though I do cut back the old fronds in early spring to better enjoy the newly emerging fronds.

'SAGAE' HOSTA

(*Hosta* 'Sagae') is a bold beauty.

Zones: 3 to 9

Size: Up to 3 feet tall and 4 feet wide

Conditions: Partial to full shade; moderately moist soil

Nothing thrills me more than seeing tightly furled hosta leaves emerging in spring. My favorite hosta, 'Sagae', is beautiful, with wavy leaves of frosted blue with creamy white margins. I grow it next to buttercup winter hazel (*Corylopsis pauciflora*, Zones 6–9), whose airy nature and delicate leaves complement the hosta's substantial size, and then pair it with green hellebore (*Helleborus* spp. and cvs., Zones 4–9) and 'Aureola' Japanese forest grass (*Hakonechloa macra* 'Aureola', Zones 5–9). 'Sagae' tolerates cold winters and never wavers in our hot and humid summers.

'SILVER SCEPTRE' SEDGE

(*Carex morrowii* 'Silver Sceptre') lends brightness to shady spots.

Zones: 5 to 9

Size: 1 foot tall and 18 inches wide

Conditions: Partial shade; moist, well-drained soil

This finely textured, fountain-shaped semi-evergreen grass lends elegance where it's planted. 'Silver Sceptre' sedge is not fussy and spreads slowly by rhizomes to form a ground cover in moderately moist soil. I like to plant it in drifts along a shady path, under the canopy of a 'Waterfall' Japanese maple (*Acer palmatum* 'Waterfall', Zones 5–8), or next to a water feature, where its fountainlike shape mimics the flow of water. This sedge only needs to be cut back by two-thirds in early spring to get it ready for new growth.

BIGROOT GERANIUM

(*Geranium macrorrhizum* and cvs.) is great for dry shade situations.

Zones: 4 to 8

Size: Up to 20 inches tall and 2 feet wide

Conditions: Full sun to partial shade; well-drained soil

It spreads quickly by rhizomes to form a dense, weed-smothering ground cover that's good for massing around trees or edging a shade border. Bigroot geranium is reliably hardy after cold winters,

and it also takes the heat of our summers when grown in shade. Once established, sharing this easy-care plant with friends is a breeze: A gentle tug releases not only a delicious scent but also a side rhizome that is ready to replant in a new garden.

—SALLY BARKER

Midwest

PURPLE CONEFLOWER

(*Echinacea purpurea* and cvs.) stands up to cold and heat.

Zones: 3 to 9

Size: Up to 5 feet tall and 3 feet wide

Conditions: Full sun to partial shade; well-drained soil

This perennial is native to our prairie, so you know it has to be tough. It is not only cold hardy and drought tolerant but also a trouper in the heat. As if that weren't enough, purple coneflower offers long-lasting summer color, makes a sturdy cut flower, and even looks handsome in winter, thanks to its large cone-shaped seed heads (which finches love). I even like the way it gently reseeds itself in my garden, filling in vacant spots.

RUGOSA ROSE

(*Rosa rugosa* and cvs.) is big on blooms and cold tolerance.

Zones: 2 to 9

Size: 4 to 6 feet tall and wide

Conditions: Full sun; well-drained soil

Modern shrub roses have given us a wide range of winter-hardy options, but I still list rugosa rose as one of my favorites. This disease-resistant species is incredibly cold tolerant, makes a great flower, and, as an added bonus, sets colorful cherry tomato–resembling hips after its blooms fade. The plant does get big, however, so keep it at the back of the border and give it plenty of room to grow.

DWARF KOREAN LILAC

(*Syringa meyeri* 'Palibin') is the perfect fit for any garden.

Zones: 4 to 7

Size: 4 to 5 feet tall and 5 to 8 feet wide

Conditions: Full sun; well-drained soil

Lilac is a reliable flowering shrub for our area, but the problem with most varieties is that they grow too big. That's why I love dwarf Korean lilac. It's the perfect size for all kinds of landscapes. It flowers reliably every spring and even starts blooming the first year—something many lilacs won't do. Best of all, it's tough. This shrub can handle just about anything our weather throws at it and comes back every year looking better than ever.

KOREANSPICE VIBURNUM

(*Viburnum carlesii*) has fantastic fragrance.

Zones: 5 to 8

Size: 6 to 8 feet tall and wide

Conditions: Full sun to partial shade; moist, well-drained soil

Few plants can rival the amazing fragrance of a Koreanspice viburnum in full bloom. For me, it's a sure sign that spring is finally here. This deciduous shrub is easy to grow and knows its place at the back of a border, kicking off spring with white flowers and then fading into the background to let summer bloomers steal the show. It always has one last hurrah in fall, however, with a blaze of red foliage.

—CAMERON REES

Southern Plains

PAINTBRUSH LILY

(*Scadoxus puniceus*, syn. *S. natalensis*) is a hardy, vibrant bloomer.

Zones: 8 to 11

Size: 20 to 30 inches tall and wide

Conditions: Partial shade; moist, well-drained soil

This stunning bulb produces large globe-shaped torches of vibrant orange flowers held high on sturdy stalks in early spring before the leaves emerge. The glossy foliage, which persists through summer and fall before going dormant, adds a whole new textural dimension to the shade. Paintbrush lily is slow to multiply and can be hard to find, but it is worth seeking out because it is so amazing.

PACO'S POSSUMHAW HOLLY

(*Ilex decidua* 'Pacos') makes for a winter-hardy friend to the birds.

Zones: 5 to 9

Size: 15 feet tall and 12 feet wide

Conditions: Full sun to partial shade; moist, well-drained soil

This is one of our favorite native ornamental trees, which can be grown as a single-trunk or multitrunk plant. Paco's possumhaw holly is a female plant that is absolutely covered with gorgeous red fruit all winter (only females produce berries). Expect birds to feast on the berries from winter into early spring. This is a tough drought-tolerant tree that can take periodic wet conditions, too—making it perfect for unpredictable winter weather.

DWARF BARBADOS CHERRY

(*Malpighia glabra* 'Nana') is fruitful.

Zones: 9 to 11

Size: 3 to 4 feet tall and wide

Conditions: Full sun to partial shade; well-drained soil

This unique, colorful native shrub is covered with pink and white flowers through summer and fall. It produces an abundance of cherrylike red fruit, which is enjoyed by a variety of birds late in the season. Its size makes it a perfect choice to use singly, in a grouping, or even as a low hedge. Dwarf Barbados cherry is evergreen in average winters and root hardy in severe winters. As a bonus, it's drought tolerant once established.

PINK SIAM TULIP GINGER

(*Curcuma alismatifolia* 'Pink') is a glorious rebloomer.

Zones: 8 to 10

Size: 1 to 2 feet tall and wide

Conditions: Full sun to partial shade; moist, well-drained soil

A tulip from Thailand? Well, not quite. This fabulous ginger has stiff, narrow leaves and elegantly erect, soft pink flowers. The long-lasting blossoms rebloom throughout summer and superficially resemble a tulip, although there is no relation. Pink Siam tulip ginger is day-length sensitive and will go dormant in late fall, returning in mid-spring as soon as the temperatures warm up. Leave some space when siting because each plant will slowly multiply.

—HEIDI SHEESLEY

Mountain West

JUPITER'S BEARD

(*Centranthus ruber*) is a durable perennial that handles our region's windy winters with grace.

Zones: 5 to 8

Size: 3 feet tall and wide

Conditions: Full sun; poor to average, well-drained soil

A milky fluid coursing through its cambium layer acts as an antifreeze during cold spells while also slowing water loss in summer. It is listed as a Zone 5 plant, but in my experience, it can survive Zone 4 winters. It produces dome-shaped clusters of dark pink flowers on 2- to 3-foot-tall stems in late spring. Expect reseeding.

PINELEAF PENSTEMON

(*Penstemon pinifolius*) is an easygoing evergreen.
Zones: 4 to 10
Size: 16 inches tall and 10 inches wide
Conditions: Full sun; well-drained soil

Pineleaf penstemon evolved to endure cold winters and hot, dry summers in nutrient-poor soils. Narrow film-covered leaves defend the plant from wind and sun by limiting water loss. When not in bloom, this evergreen sits only 4 to 5 inches above the ground to further minimize exposure to the elements. For brilliant performance, water and fertilize sparingly. This may seem counterintuitive, but pineleaf penstemon wants to be shunned. It rewards neglect with scarlet and orange tubular flowers in early summer. Afterward, the foliage resembles that of a pine.

CREEPING MAHONIA

(*Mahonia repens*) thumbs its nose at winter and provides four-season interest.
Zones: 5 to 8
Size: 1 foot tall and 3 feet wide
Conditions: Full sun to partial shade; moist, well-drained soil

To survive, the leaves of this evergreen subshrub feature a water-conserving waxy coat that can make or break a plant in our Mountain West winters; those evergreen leaves also hold snow around the plant as insulation. In spring, creeping mahonia produces bright yellow flowers that contrast nicely with its dark green leaves. These flowers are followed by deep blue berries at the end of summer. In late autumn, the leaves turn a beautiful burgundy red and last through winter.

PARTRIDGE FEATHER

(*Tanacetum densum* ssp. *amani*) has foliage that resembles—you guessed it—the plumage of a partridge.
Zones: 4 to 9
Size: Up to 10 inches tall and 15 inches wide
Conditions: Full sun; sandy, well-drained soil

This ground cover's silvery blue color helps dissipate heat from intense sunlight, and the fuzzy filaments on the leaves reduce water loss. Keep partridge feather under dry conditions. I made the mistake of watering it once a week in summer, and it perished. I now never give it a drink, and it thrives.

—TOM HEALD

Northern California

GERMANDER

(*Teucrium chamaedrys*) takes to borders and edges.
Zones: 4 to 9
Size: 1 to 2 feet tall and 3 feet wide
Conditions: Full sun; well-drained soil

Germander is an aromatic, drought-tolerant, deer-resistant perennial that nicely overwinters here. It's a wonderful border or edging plant, and it is often used in knot gardens and around formal garden displays. Left to sprawl, the plants become intertwined, creating a solid pink carpet. I especially love the look of germander in early spring, when the gray-green leaves are young and the clumps are mounded.

'GULF STREAM' HEAVENLY BAMBOO

(*Nandina domestica* 'Gulf Stream') shines year-round.
Zones: 6 to 11
Size: Up to 42 inches tall and 3 feet wide
Conditions: Full sun to partial shade; prefers sandy loam with good drainage but tolerates most soils

This hardy and virtually pest- and disease-free semi-dwarf evergreen heavenly bamboo performs beautifully year-round. A compact, mounded habit; moderately fast growth; and intense red fall color make 'Gulf Stream' one of the best heavenly bamboos you'll find in northern California. It's drought tolerant and deer resistant, and it tolerates heavy frost. Use this plant along a foundation, or plant it in swaths for color interest and seasonal impact. It's a perfect fit for any garden style.

LARGE CAPE RUSH

(*Chondropetalum elephantinum*) is architectural and fluid.
Zones: 9 to 11
Size: 4 to 6 feet tall and wide
Conditions: Full sun to partial shade; well-drained soil

A South African native, this variety of Cape rush is similar to the more common small Cape rush (*C. tectorum*, Zones 9–11), only larger. The vertical grasslike stems of large Cape rush have dark green joints and mahogany bracts, and they form an elegant clump with a striking architectural structure, which works well with vertical hardscapes or as a stand-alone focal point. It's evergreen in northern California, and it is deer resistant. I love how the reeds move with the wind. I often plant large Cape rush against a stucco- or stone-wall backdrop to highlight its superb form.

JERUSALEM SAGE

(*Phlomis fruticosa*) has a structural presence.

Zones: 7 to 11

Size: 6 feet tall and 4 feet wide

Conditions: Full sun; well-drained soil

Jerusalem sage begins its performance in mid-spring, continues well into summer, and often blooms again in fall. I have deadheaded it after it blooms, but sometimes I just leave it alone to do its own thing—and I still get a great repeat performance. I love how it overwinters, always keeping a structural presence in the garden while other plants are resting in dormancy. Plant Jerusalem sage in large swaths on terraces or slopes, or pair it with clusters of deep purple–flowered 'Eleanor Roosevelt' bearded iris (*Iris* 'Eleanor Roosevelt', Zones 3–9).

—SUSIE DOWD MARKARIAN

Northwest

'SPARKLING BURGUNDY' PINEAPPLE LILY

(*Eucomis comosa* 'Sparkling Burgundy') has merlot-colored leaves.

Zones: 8 to 11

Size: 18-inch-tall foliage (with 30-inch-tall flowering stems) and 2 feet wide

Conditions: Full sun to partial shade; rich, well-drained soil

Visitors to our garden always notice this South African bulb, especially in early summer, when its merlot-colored leaves emerge. Although 'Sparkling Burgundy' pineapple lily looks tropical, it's unquestionably hardy. Some *Eucomis* species are tender or slow to establish, but all varieties of *E. comosa* are reliable in our climate. For the darkest foliage color, give this perennial a sunny spot.

GIANT FEATHER GRASS

(*Stipa gigantea*) is a vigorous favorite.

Zones: 8 to 11

Size: 8 feet tall and 6 feet wide

Conditions: Full sun; poor to average, well-drained soil

If I had to list my top five favorite ornamental grasses, giant feather grass would certainly make the cut. This cool-season grass is drought tolerant, deer resistant, low maintenance, and cold hardy. Once the dry days of summer commence in western Oregon, usually around July 4, the green seed heads on this grass age to a golden straw color, which shimmers beautifully in the afternoon sun. If the plant's vigor starts to wane over time, simply divide the aging clumps in late winter.

'PURPLE SMOKE' FALSE INDIGO

(*Baptisia* 'Purple Smoke') thrives on "tough love."

Zones: 3 to 9

Size: 4 feet tall and wide

Conditions: Full sun; lean, well-drained soil

If the soil is too rich or too moist, the plant flops right over. Neglect this North American native, however, and you'll have dusky purple flowers on sturdy gray-colored stems through most of summer, followed by a shapely shrublike plant with ornamental seedpods for the rest of the season. 'Purple Smoke' false indigo, like many *Baptisia* cultivars, is hardy to –40°F, the likes of which have never been seen in our valley. Plus, it's deer resistant.

SIERRA MADRE LOBELIA

(*Lobelia laxiflora* var. *angustifolia*) is bird and bee friendly.

Zones: 8 to 10

Size: 2 feet tall and wide

Conditions: Full sun; rich, well-drained soil

I never would have guessed that a plant native to the American Southwest would handle our wet winters so well. I love this plant—and so do the hummingbirds and bees. All summer, Sierra Madre lobelia features a long-lasting show of scarlet flowers without any deadheading. At the close of the season, simply trim it back after the first hard frost. This is a low-maintenance, trouble-free plant. But it likes rich soil, so be sure to give it a yearly dose of compost.

—LEONARD FOLTZ

Tomatoes

—STEVE AITKEN

Choose the right staking method for you.

Cages Support Side Branches

Pros:	Cons:
Good support for branches	Not sturdy
	Not attractive
	Not much support for main stem

Tepees are as Tall as You Make Them

Pros:	Cons:
Sturdy	Require a lot of space
Inexpensive	Need to be built
Easy to adapt	
Tall enough for any tomato	

Spirals Look Good

Pros:	Cons:
Cool looks	Too short for most tomatoes
Strong support for main stem	No support for side branches
	Can lean due to weight from plant

Ladders are Less Likely to Lean

Pros:	Cons:
Strong support for main stem	Expensive
Some support for side branches	One stake is often not tall enough
Can be stacked for greater height	Side stems can break or tangle due to lack of support

Tie 'Em Up

Many supports allow you to wind the main stem through it, but you will occasionally need to tie it or some side branches to your stake. Options abound, from homemade (fabric scraps, such as nylon ties) to commercial (tomato clips). Whatever you use, a good tie will not abrade the stem, nor will it girdle the stem as it grows.

When it comes to supporting a multitude of side branches, a cage can be an outstanding choice. But it isn't the most attractive option, nor is it the sturdiest. Adding some wooden stakes down the sides helps a cage stay upright and may—or may not—add to its appearance.

A ladder provides as much support to the main stem as a spiral but lends more support for side branches. It is also less likely to lean under the weight of the plant. Like a spiral, however, it is often too short to do the job. Many tomato ladders, fortunately, can stand on top of one another, providing the height to hold a huge tomato plant.

A spiral is designed to let you wind the main stem around it, providing support. It also looks great in late spring before it gets covered in foliage. The problems with a spiral are that it isn't nearly tall enough to handle an indeterminate tomato and it offers no support to side stems.

Potentially the tallest of supports, a tepee can be built out of almost anything: from bamboo stakes to found branches. Its shape makes it sturdy, but you will need to provide some support for side branches either by adding side braces or by spiraling twine around the structure. Plant tomatoes at the base of each pole or grow one plant in the center; in that case, a center pole might be required for support.

Create a Living Wall of Tomatoes

—SCOTT DAIGRE

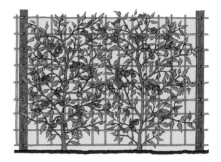

If you happen to have a sturdy wire fence around or near your vegetable garden, you can use it to support your tomatoes and create a living wall. After planting against the bottom of the fence, tie off the branches as they grow, spreading them wider and wider to give each of the leaves the maximum amount of exposure to the sun. Attach the branches with soft ties, hook-and-loop tape, or twine.

Some Snap Peas Need a Trellis; Others Don't

—DAVID HIRSCH

I grow my 'Sugar Snap' peas on a simple trellis, which runs down the center of a raised bed. The heavy, pea-laden vines grow up to 7 feet tall, and they need a substantial support to keep them from blowing over. While it takes a little extra work to set up a trellis, I appreciate the comfort of not having to harvest every vegetable squatting, crouching, or bending over (see the illustration on the facing page).

You don't need a trellis to grow some varieties of snap peas. Good-tasting dwarf varieties, like 'Sugar Ann' or 'Sugar Bon', require little or no help to hold themselves off the ground. Their vines grow 18 to 24 inches tall and bear 2½-inch-long pods about 60 days after planting. The pods are ready to harvest a week to 10 days earlier than 'Sugar Snap' peas.

A Simple Trellis of Fence and Twine

—BECKY BLADES

On a privacy-type fence—with vertical boards that have nothing for twining vines to grasp on to—make a simple trellis support. Tie a knot in the end of a length of twine, slip the knot between the boards, and slide it down to a cross board. Do this with five or six more lengths of twine, sliding them between every other board. Then gather all the ends together and tie them into a simple knot near the ground, resulting in a fan of string from the ground to near the top of the fence. Hammer a 1- to 2-foot-long 2x2 stake, with a ½-inch-deep groove near the top, into the ground where you want to anchor the trellis. Slip the knot over the stake and into the groove, which holds the twine in place. Trim the ends of the strings and give the stake an additional tap with the hammer to pull it all tight. This simple vine support is great for reseeded annual vines or perennial vines that are pruned back to the ground each year.

Give an Old Tree Branch a New Job

—TODD MEIER

Rather than buy another trellis, I cut a dead but shapely branch out of an old apple tree near my house and inserted it into a container to use as a structure on which to grow annual vines. By midsummer, the branch was transformed into a red and green globe covered in cardinal climber vines. It also became a conversation piece among my neighbors. I've saved the branch to use next year with a different type of annual vine.

Train Wisteria to Climb

—MEGHAN RAY

To begin training a new plant onto a pergola or arbor, allow two or three young shoots to twine loosely around each other and the post as they grow. This will help to provide added interest to the plant's structure, since the woody stems become contorted and picturesque with maturity. The young shoots need to be secured to the post as they climb. To do this, attach a 14-gauge galvanized (or similar) wire using eye hooks, spaced about 18 inches apart, along two opposite sides of the post (or on all four sides for extra support). As the shoots grow, tie them as needed to the wire using gardening twine. Allow some slack as they grow to create a more attractive habit and to prevent the plant from putting heavy tension on the structure as the plant matures.

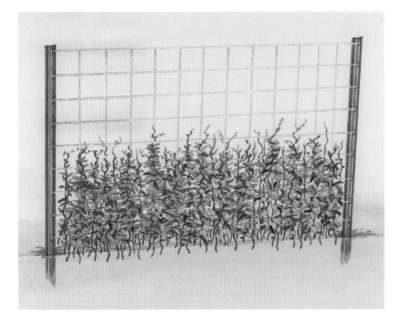

BUILD A SIMPLE TRELLIS

You can set up an inexpensive 8-foot-long trellis in less than an hour. You'll need two 7-foot-tall metal fence posts and an 8-foot length of nylon trellis netting.

- Pound the posts 2 feet into the ground. Then string the netting between them, stretching it tight and tying at even intervals up and down the sides. Pea-laden vines are heavy, so make sure the netting is attached securely.

- Cut the vines at the base of the trellis at the end of the season, and let them dry out. Pull the dried vines off the netting, and bring the netting inside for winter.

- Reuse the same netting for up to 10 years. You can also use bio-degradable netting instead of nylon so that you can cut the mesh and pea vines down together and compost the whole thing.

—DAVID HIRSCH

PRUNE

GENERAL TIPS FOR PLANTS

If You Hate to Prune . . .
—KERRY A. MENDEZ

Let's face it. Pruning and deadheading are necessary evils, but ones we have control over. To reduce time spent on these laborious tasks, I choose shrubs that require little or no pruning and herbaceous plants that bloom without my assistance. Avoid woody plants that sucker or are persnickety, such as lilacs (*Syringa* spp. and cvs., Zones 3–8) and hybrid roses (*Rosa* cvs., Zones 4–11). Likewise, select herbaceous plants that have a long bloom without deadheading. Some terrific perennials to consider are butterfly weeds (*Asclepias* spp. and cvs., Zones 3–11), sneezeweeds (*Helenium* spp. and cvs., Zones 4–8), and bugbanes (*Actaea* spp. and cvs., Zones 4–9). The annual contingent includes calibrachoas (*Calibrochoa* cvs.), impatiens (*Impatiens* spp. and cvs.), and *vincas* (*Catharanthus roseus* cvs.).

Deadhead a Plant
—FINE GARDENING EDITORS

No, this doesn't mean you dress up your favorite plant in tie-dye and rock out to the Grateful Dead. We're talking flowers and seed heads here. Deadheading means you cut off spent blooms to prevent a plant from going to seed too quickly. This will, in most cases, force the plant into a second round of lush blooms.

Pinching a Plant Is an Act of Kindness
—FINE GARDENING EDITORS

Pinching a plant almost feels mean: It has just put out all this nice new growth, and you're taking it away. But the rewards are worth the sacrifice. Many plants benefit from a good pinching in spring. They become stronger, bushier plants as a result—for whenever you pinch back one stem, two stems will emerge from the node left behind. You might even be able to root the stems you pinched off, which means more plants for you. If you're doubtful, try this simple experiment. Buy two identical coleus (*Solenostemon scutellarioides* cvs., Zones 12–13) plants in spring. Pinch one plant, but leave the other alone. Compare the two plants in August, and decide for yourself.

The Kindest Cut

—LEE REICH

When pruning trees and shrubs, always make an angled cut just above and sloping away from a viable bud. Buds are located immediately above the point where a leaf is attached to a branch or, if the plant is dormant and leafless, above the leaf scar (a mark left on a branch where the leaf was once attached). Be careful not to cut too close to the bud. This will damage the bud, causing it to dry out and die—leaving a dead stub. And don't cut too far above a bud, either, because the stub that remains will eventually die, rot away, and provide a possible entryway for disease.

CORRECT
Cut is made just beyond bud and at an angle.

INCORRECT
Cut is made too close to bud. Bud will dry out.

INCORRECT
Cut is made too far from bud. Dead stub will remain.

The Best Time to Prune Trees

—JOHN BALL

Generally speaking, the best time to conduct tree pruning is during late winter. Insect and disease problems are rare during this time, and the tree quickly recovers. It is also easier to see what needs to be pruned when the leaves are absent. If only a branch or two needs to be removed, however, almost any time will do. Oaks are an exception. If you live in an area where oak wilt is a problem, do not prune those trees during May, June, or July because the pruning wound may attract insects carrying the disease. The same is true for a number of other pests, so it is always a good idea to check with a local tree expert or master gardener to see if there are any times not to prune your particular tree.

JAPANESE MAPLES

Let It Age

Japanese maples less than 15 years old are prone to put on new growth that looks like a buggy whip: unattractively skinny with no side branches. This problem is exacerbated by pruning, often done by the impatient tree owner hoping to create an open look sooner than nature intended. Shortening or removing the buggy whips only stimulates more of the same. My best advice is to leave the tree alone for as long as possible. You will be surprised to find that, as the whips age, they fatten up, develop lateral branches, and turn into nice-looking scaffold limbs. Trust me. Sit on your hands and wait to start the thinning process until after the tree has aged and developed some grace.

Let It Grow

Avoid attempting to restrict the height of a Japanese maple. It won't work. The tree will simply grow faster with thin, unruly branches. The width of these trees, on the other hand, can be somewhat modified.

Almost Anytime Is the Right Time to Prune

But you must prune Japanese maples selectively. With that said, these maples are most easily pruned in winter or summer. With the leaves out of the way in winter, it is easy to see the branch structure and, in turn, make the right cuts. In summer, however, you can judge the right amount of thinning needed to see the tree's bones. Summer pruning also stimulates less plant growth than winter pruning, so you can get away with a little more and the tree will stay thinned out longer. I avoid pruning when the temperature is 80°F or higher, especially when the plant is located in full sun. Removing foliage will expose the tree's thin, previously shaded bark to the light, inviting sunscald.

Go Lightly on the Crown and Branches

To avoid causing stress or stimulating unsightly growth, never remove more than one-fifth of a Japanese maple's crown; you should also not prune a branch that is more than half the diameter of the parent stem. In addition, don't remove more than a quarter of the foliage of any given branch. Each branch is fed by its leaves through photosynthesis.

If you are going to "limb up" your tree by pruning the lowest branches, avoid stress to the plant by removing only a few at a time, not many at once. Never make one cut directly above the other or opposite another limb being pruned off in the same year. That might cause decay to coalesce inside the trunk.

Separate the Branches into Overlapping Layers That Don't Touch Each Other

This is the trick to making Japanese maples look great. Most single-stemmed plants have a series of scaffold branches that radiate in a roughly spiral fashion up the trunk. If a lateral branch from any of these scaffolds grows downward, crossing into the layer below, it should be removed or cut back to a side branch facing up and out. This is how the tree becomes layered, like a series of fans.

Give the Parent Stem Room

When pruning a Japanese maple, cut up to—but not into—the branch collar. If you cut too far out, you will leave an unsightly stub. If you cut too close to the parent stem (a flush cut), a column of rot will enter the stem. To minimize stress, dieback, and regrowth, do not remove a side branch that exceeds half the diameter of the parent stem.

Accept the Shape of Your Tree

Some Japanese maples do not have especially graceful branches, possessing instead a twiggy or stiff-looking internal structure. Pruning cannot change the essential character of these trees. The wise gardener learns to appreciate plants for their own attributes and remembers that a good pruner can only reveal beauty, not create it.

—CASS TURNBULL

Should You Cover Newly Pruned Areas With Varnish, Tar, or Paint?

—JOHN C. FETCH

There really isn't a way to keep fungal organisms out of a new cut. In about half of the situations where these wound dressings are used, the tree's heartwood decays faster than it would have without the topical application. The paint or tar holds moisture near the new wound, which, unfortunately, helps the various fungal decay organisms grow. Instead, simply make a clean cut just outside the branch collar and leave it alone. If pruned properly, trees can take advantage of natural defense mechanisms to ward off most decay problems.

Prune Dead Wood to Thwart Disease

—LEE REICH

For branches that are ailing or dead, the best practice is to make a cut about 6 inches into live, healthy wood (usually evident by the presence of viable buds). Some diseases spread within a plant; by cutting off the diseased part, you stop the advance of the disease. If you are not sure if a branch is dead or alive, gently scrape the bark with your pruners to reveal the color of the growth layer underneath. Green means that it's still alive. Brown means it's time to prune. To further avoid the spread of disease, dip your pruning tools in alcohol or a 10 percent bleach solution between cuts.

In the case of a broken branch or a pair of rubbing branches, simply make a clean cut back either to a crotch (an area where the branch meets another branch or trunk) or to the nearest bud.

Thin Crowded Stems to Encourage New Growth

—LEE REICH

First, remove old, decrepit stems that have declined in flower production and have grown too tall (the age at which this happens varies from species to species, so take note of your plant's performance each year). Prune any candidates back to ground level or to a vigorous shoot near the stem base. This will allow more light into the center of the plant, triggering new shoots to grow. Next, remove some of the youngest stems so that the remaining stems have room to grow. Keep in mind that some shrubs grow more new stems from ground level each year than others; the more new stems that grow, the more stems that will need to be thinned out annually. Shrub thinning should be done regularly so that the shrub will uniformly renew itself over time.

Remove Suckers at Growing Points
—LEE REICH

The best way to remove suckers—vigorous vertical stems that ruin a tree's appearance—is to get them while they're young (under ¼ inch in diameter) and during the early part of the growing season. Simply grab them and give a sharp yank sideways, ripping them away at their growing point. If the suckers are too old to yank off, they must be cut off as close to the growing point as possible. If a sucker is not removed all the way back to its growing point, new suckers will grow from the base of the old one.

CONIFERS

There is no place for recreational pruning of conifers because they don't replace growth like other trees and shrubs. Here are some identification tips, timing guidelines, and pruning methods for the most common conifers.
—BERT CREGG

Pruning Method for Arborvitae, Juniper, and Chamaecyparis
Unlike some conifers, these trees will not form new buds on old wood. So if you cut back to the brown, aged stems, the tree won't grow back. Pruning for size control, therefore, can only be done on new growth (where the stems are still green and pliable). Snip branch tips back lightly, when the plant is pushing new growth in late spring or early summer.

Pruning Method for Hemlock and Yew
To help shape these trees into formal hedges or to encourage fullness, lightly trim back the outermost growth using hand pruners or hedge shears. These conifers get a flush of new growth after pruning, so the best time to give them a haircut is when they are not actively growing, in late winter or late summer.

Pruning Method for Pine
Pines should be pruned during active shoot growth, in late spring, because this will allow sufficient time for the shoot to produce a new set of buds for next year's growth. The current year's new shoots, or "candles," can be cut with hand pruners or simply pinched off to the desired length.

Pruning Method for Fir, Douglas Fir, and Spruce
To control height, prune the leader while the trees are dormant. These conifers form buds along their stems, so make a cut half an inch or so above a bud. The topmost bud will become the new leader. This cut will also stimulate outward growth of the buds below. Lightly trimming back the outermost branch tips during dormancy (in late winter or late summer) will also encourage fullness when the tree pushes new growth in spring.

THREE METHODS TO PRUNE THE "UNPRUNABLES"

You know the offenders: forsythia, elderberry, and beautybush, just to name a few. It seems that no one knows exactly how to prune this rogue group, but, if left alone, these plants look gangly and unkempt. I suggest using one of three alternative pruning methods. Each has its pros and cons, but every one will leave your shrub looking better.

—PAUL CAPPIELLO

The Busy Banker Buzz Cut

If you happen to be one of those people who might not have time to tweak and primp the shrubs in your garden, I suggest the every-three-year whack because it's quick and easy. Simply ignore the shrub for three years and then, one day in late winter or early spring, run home, fire up the chain saw, and buzz the beast to within 6 inches of the ground. Then stand back and watch your shrub explode with new growth as soon as the weather warms up.

Pros:

The plant will rebound quickly, and the following year, it will have a more uniform and compact habit and the bloom set will be better.

Cons:

You'll lose the flowers for one spring on those species that set them on old wood: elderberry, deutzia, mock orange, flowering quince, and forsythia.

The Structured Engineer Shear

This approach celebrates rules and systems—the notion that there is a way a plant should grow and look and that it's a gardener's job to ensure that order is maintained. The goal is to have a shrub with evenly spaced branches and balanced branch distribution. You must adopt this method when the plant is young and plan on spending a pruning session in summer and in winter—every year—selecting, envisioning, and clipping all crossing branches. With fast-growing, suckering shrubs like the unprunables, this takes a Herculean effort but creates a spectacular specimen.

Pros:

The considerable upside is that, with these shrubs, there is simply no other way to achieve a beautiful, sculptural focal point plant in the garden.

Cons:

It takes time—lots and lots of time.

The Surfer Dude Trim

This pruning style is best suited to gardeners who like hanging out in the hammock, admiring their garden, rather than obsessively pulling the weeds within it. Here's how to do it: If you happen to notice a wild branch that seems out of place, give it a snip. Trimming can be done at any time of year and requires little effort. Don't worry about those pesky crossing branches—just clip a few bits here and there to give the shrub the shape you like.

Pros:

Small bits of pruning like this can be done, as they say, "anytime the shears are sharp." If you are only removing partial branches here and there, you won't be likely to trigger the plant to force tons of regrowth as you might with aggressive renewal pruning or heavy shearing. This means there is no risk of frost damage if trimming in early spring or in fall.

Cons:

Your shrub will never be considered an architectural masterpiece, and it may eventually become so dense that its inner branches begin to die from lack of light.

Wisteria

—MEGHAN RAY

In Summer, Wait Until the Flowers Fade

Since wisteria flowers develop on the previous year's growth, pruning wisterias biannually not only keeps these vigorous vines to a manageable size but also creates a system of short branches close to the structure, where you can more easily enjoy the blooms. To accomplish this, simply prune the long shoots of the current year's growth back to 6 inches long in early summer after the vines have flowered. Also at this time, completely remove any shoots not needed for the main framework of the plant and prune away root suckers, especially on grafted varieties. This type of pruning may be done once a summer or more frequently, depending on how much time you have and how neat you want your vine to look. Keep in mind that many gardeners find wisteria seedpods decorative, so you many want to leave some spent flowers behind.

In Winter, Prune Long Shoots

In late winter, prune the long shoots that have grown since the summer pruning down to three to five buds. Also remove any of last season's unwanted long shoots, which will be more apparent now because the leafless framework will be exposed. Even short branches should be cut to three to five buds to direct energy to flower production rather than vegetative growth.

Subshrubs

—DEBRA KNAPKE

Don't Treat Your Lavender as You Would Your Herbaceous Plants

When it comes to subshrubs (such as lavender, periwinkle, and thyme), it's a good idea not to cut them back to the ground, since this can result in the removal of their growing points and can ultimately lead to their demise. Similarly, the worst time to prune is during the cool (or potentially fluctuating) temperatures of fall and winter. The tender new growth induced by pruning is likely to be damaged or killed when cold winter temperatures arrive. The loss of the energy expended on the new growth can exhaust the plant, causing it to lose its vigor or die. Depending on the type of subshrub, the best times to prune are in the spring and, in some cases, after the first bloom. During the cooler seasons, limit your pruning to the removal of spent blossoms and dead branches and avoid cutting into live woody stems. Since their new growth is particularly sensitive to cold temperatures, tender new growth is damaged or killed by frosty temperatures, and the plant loses vigor or dies since its energy reserves are spent.

WEED

EASY STEPS TO BANISH WEEDS

Let Sleeping Weeds Lie

—BARBARA PLEASANT

Every square inch of your garden contains weed seeds, but only those in the top inch or two of soil get enough light to trigger germination. Digging and cultivating bring hidden weed seeds to the surface, so assume weed seeds are there ready to erupt, like ants from an upset anthill, every time you open a patch of ground. Dig only when you need to and immediately salve the disturbed spot with plants or mulch. In lawns, minimize soil disturbance by using a sharp knife with a narrow blade to slice through the roots of dandelions and other lawn weeds to sever their feed source rather than digging them out. Keep in mind that weed seeds can remain dormant for a long, long time.

Mulch, Mulch, Mulch

—*FINE GARDENING* EDITORS

Mulch benefits plants by keeping the soil cool and moist and depriving weeds of light. Organic mulches, in particular, can actually host crickets and carabid beetles, which seek out and devour thousands of weed seeds. Some light passes through chunky mulches, and often you will discover—too late—that the mulch you used was laced with weed seeds. It's important to replenish the mulch as needed to keep it about 2 inches deep (more than 3 inches deep can deprive soil of oxygen).

Newspaper, Cardboard, and Landscape Fabric Can Help

—BARBARA PLEASANT

You can set weeds way back by covering the soil's surface with a light-blocking sheet of cardboard, newspaper, or biodegradable fabric and then spreading prettier mulch over it. If you choose to use this method on seldom-dug areas, such as the root zones of shrubs and trees, opt for tough landscape fabric for the light-blocking bottom sheet. There is a catch, however: As soon as enough organic matter accumulates on the landscape fabric, weed seeds dropped by birds or carried in on the wind will start to grow. For the bottom layer of fabric to be effective, these must be pulled before they sink their roots through and into the ground.

PICK & PRESERVE

Keep Your Garden Basket Light to Carry the Load
—JEFF TAYLOR

A lightweight garden basket allows you to pluck and port all kinds of produce out of the garden in big batches. Typical containers for the purpose include wicker baskets, wooden trugs, canvas totes, rubber buckets, flexible tubs made of heavy-gauge polyethylene, and spring-loaded vinyl baskets that hold themselves open like a hippo's mouth. I prefer a really big container for most harvesting jobs, herbs, flowers, berries, and tomatoes aside. But a shallow wooden trug is designed to keep soft fruit from getting crushed.

Harvest Flower Seeds Easily
—FINE GARDENING EDITORS

It's best to let seeds ripen on plants until they are almost ready to disperse on their own. A seed harvested too early will not be viable. Seeds usually change color (from light to dark) when they are ready to be harvested. Cut off the entire stem containing the spent flower head or the entire pod containing the seed. Take seeds indoors to a cool, dry spot to let them finish ripening inside a closed paper bag.

Three Ways to Preserve Your Herbs
—JENNIFER BENNER

1. Drying is often the preserving method of choice because it is quick and easy, and some herbs, like oregano, are more flavorful when dried. Herbs can be hung to dry, laid out on a drying screen, or dried in an oven or dehydrator. After drying, store the leaves in a glass jar in a dark, dry, cool place.

2. Freezing often delivers the same flavor as fresh—the leaves just take a beating and lose their crispness. Chopped fresh leaves can be frozen directly in freezer bags, in ice-cube trays (with water), or as a paste (herbs mixed with olive oil) stored in a freezer-proof container.

3. Add them to vinegars. This is for all you salad lovers out there. Adding herbs to vinegar is a great way to continue to enjoy your herbal bounty. Wine vinegars work well with herbs without overpowering them. Choose a white-wine vinegar if seeing the color of the herb, such as 'Red Rubin' basil, is important to you. Here are the basics: Clean the herbs, add some vinegar, store in a jar for two to four weeks (shaking daily and occasionally checking for taste), strain into a new clean jar, and enjoy.

10 Outstanding Herbs for Tea

—CARY WALL

1. Bee balm leaves and flowers (*Monarda didyma* and cvs., Zones 4–9)
2. Cinnamon basil leaves (*Ociumum basilicum* 'Cinnamon Basil', annual)
3. German chamomile flowers in full bloom (*Matricaria recutita*, annual)
4. Lemon balm leaves (*Melissa officinalis*, Zones 3–7)
5. Lemon thyme leaves and stems (*Thymus × citriodorus*, Zones 6–9)
6. Peppermint leaves and stems (*Mentha × piperita*, Zones 3–7)
7. Raspberry leaves (*Rubus strigosus*, Zones 4–8)
8. Rose petals and hips (*Rosa* spp. and cvs., Zones 3–9)
9. Spearmint leaves and stems (*Mentha spicata*, Zones 3–7)
10. Wild strawberry leaves (*Fragaria vesca*, Zones 5–9)

....

Pick Ripe Raspberries Often

—JAY LESHINSKY

When your raspberries are still firm but separate easily from the plant, it's time to harvest. Ripe berries go by quickly, so they should be picked at least every day or two. I put the berries into pint containers so that the berries are not crushed. Wet berries are prone to rot, so I gather them when they're dry and I don't wash them. Those that make it into the house (rather than into my mouth) go right into the refrigerator unless I'm going to eat them within a few hours. Those I don't eat within a day or two after picking, I freeze.

....

KNOW WHEN TO HARVEST . . .

Tomatoes

Pick tomatoes when they have colored up, when the flesh gives to gentle pressure, and when the stem willingly separates from the vine at the first joint above the fruit. Color is the first indication that a tomato is nearing ripeness, but the other two clues are better signs.

Corn

Corn silks turning dry and brown indicate that the kernels inside are full and milky and ready to harvest. This generally happens about three weeks after the silks first begin to show.

Winter Squash

Leave winter squash on the vine until the rind has hardened and its color has deepened. If you plan to store them, leave them on the vine until the plant has died, then pick the fruit.

Eggplants and Peppers

These can be picked once the fruit has reached a usable size, but be sure to harvest eggplants while the skin is still glossy, because once it dulls, the quality diminishes. And if you're after red peppers, leave them until they've fully colored up.

Summer Squash

These can be eaten at any size but are best when relatively small and tender. Pick while the skin is still glossy and has some "grab" when you move your hand across it.

Green Beans and Cucumbers

These can be picked when they're the size you want. Just don't let them get too large. Pick shelling peas as soon as the peas have filled out the pod.

Leeks and Onions

These can be pulled and eaten at any stage. Leave onions intended for storage in the ground until their tops yellow.

Garlic

Garlic is ready when the tops are starting to yellow but they still have five or six green leaves.

Potatoes

You can start digging for *new potatoes* about seven weeks after the plants break ground. For *storage potatoes*, wait until two weeks after the plants have died before digging.

Other Root Vegetables

Beets, turnips, and carrots can be harvested when you like the size, but you'll need to do some prospecting to determine when your treasures are big enough to suit you.

Leafy Vegetables

Pick lettuces, spinach, and greens leaf by leaf or head by head, whenever they're big enough for you.

—RUTH LIVELY

PART FIVE

PESTS, BENEFICIAL INSECTS
& disease

PESTS

INTEGRATED PEST MANAGEMENT (IPM)

IPM Is an Approach With a Long View

—RICHARD DEVINE

Integrated Pest Management (IPM) is a way to control pests that doesn't rely heavily on chemicals. This approach stresses monitoring pest populations and using natural and artificial controls to keep pest and disease damage from reaching unacceptably high levels. While it's been used frequently in agriculture for several decades, it's also becoming popular among ornamental gardeners. By practicing IPM, you take a long view on encouraging plant health and solving plant problems.

Practice the Principles of IPM

—RICHARD DEVINE

Begin with Careful Plant Selection and Placement

Choosing the right plants is critical. Since many pests prey on specific plant genuses or species, planting trouble-prone plants invites more work and disappointment. Sometimes it's just a matter of doing a little hunting to find the most resilient plants for your conditions. For example, I've replaced some of my finicky hybrid roses with more trouble-free species roses.

Of course, plants perform best when they're given the right type of soil, moisture, nutrients, and light, as well as enough room to grow. It's also essential to use mulch to suppress weeds, and, if necessary, to weed by hand. Plants enduring less-than-ideal conditions can become stressed and susceptible to pests and diseases.

Since IPM involves limiting the use of pesticides, it's important to clearly define the function of the garden or landscaping. Is it a front yard that should look shipshape at all times or is it a more casual naturalistic garden? How much plant damage will make the landscape look unappealing? While a few chewed leaves might go unnoticed, a shrub with a veil of powdery mildew might look too unsightly.

Keep an Eye on Your Plants

Monitor your plants to find ways to promote their health in the long term rather than taking drastic, short-term measures, which often can lead to more problems.

Monitoring can be as simple as a weekly walk-through of the garden. Look for anything out of the ordinary and examine any plants with signs of stress, such as yellowed or damaged leaves. Use simple aids, such as sticky yellow cards, that help alert you to the presence of specific insects. This gives you a good sense of the ebb and flow of insect populations and whether their presence is becoming a real threat.

When you come across a problem, use a garden log to record the symptoms, such as leaf, stem, and root abnormalities. Also note all cultural conditions under which the plant is being grown. This way you can track a problem over time and see if symptoms recur from year to year.

By observing the symptoms and diagnosing the problem (see "Ask These Seven Questions to Diagnose What Made Your Good Plant Go Bad," p. 220), I can usually tell whether the problem is related to culture, a pest, or disease.

Start a Course of Treatment

If the problem seems to stem from improper culture, you can modify the plant's environment. If the problem is a pest or disease, you must decide how to treat the problem. Options include physical traps and barriers, biological controls such as horticultural oils, or chemical pesticides. In most cases, I use the least toxic means of control first, before proceeding to more drastic measures.

TREATMENT OPTIONS FOR PESTS AND DISEASES

Integrated Pest Management (IPM) relies on taking the least toxic approach to a problem and increasing the severity of treatment only if the problem persists at unacceptable levels. This chart summarizes the most common types of controls for pest and disease problems.

—RICHARD DEVINE

Nontoxic Controls

- Change cultural conditions: light, water, soil pH and fertility, or mulch.

- Correct nutrient deficiencies or excesses.

- Adjust maintenance: Remove or mow weeds, avoid leaving plants wet after sundown, and prune to increase air circulation.

- Tolerate some leaf damage, often up to 20 or 30 percent, and allow plants to recover naturally over time.

- Be careful with garden hygiene: Remove and dispose of diseased or infested plants or plant parts; clean up and compost garden debris in the fall.

- Use physical controls, such as traps, barriers, detection tools, and removal of pests by hand or with water spray.

- Try biological controls (organisms that limit pests): natural predators, parasites, nematodes, fungi, bacteria, and beneficial viruses. Avoid using chemicals that kill such organisms.

Less Toxic Controls

- Use controls that target specific taxonomic groups, eating habits, or life stages: insecticidal soaps, horticultural oils, pheromones, and growth-regulating natural substances such as neem oil.

- Select target-specific synthetic pesticides: insecticides, fungicides, herbicides, and bactericides. These often must be applied at a specific point in the life cycle of the pest or disease.

- Use systemic and preemergent synthetic chemicals (substances that can suppress problems before they emerge).

Most Toxic Controls

- As a last resort, consider using broad-spectrum chemical poisons. These, however, kill organisms indiscriminately upon contact and can cause harm to the environment or to you and others. Thus, they should be used with extreme care.

BEETLES

A Recipe to Kill Potato Beetles

—FINE GARDENING EDITORS

Colorado potato beetles (*Leptinotarsa decemlineata*) munch away on the leaves of potato plants (their favorite), tomatoes, eggplants, peppers, and similar crops until there is almost nothing left. This leaf damage causes the plant either to produce fewer fruit, vegetables, or tubers or to flat-out croak.

So what is an environmentally conscious gardener to do? Scott Endres and Dean Engelmann, of Tangletown Gardens in Minneapolis, recommend that when you see these pests, you should sprinkle a mixture of talcum powder (baby powder) and flour over your plants. When this moisture-sapping mix is ingested, it dries out the beetles' outer mucus layer, which ultimately leads to death. This leaves you with a healthy crop and no more potato beetles.

Potato beetle
(*Leptinotarsa decemlineata*)

Beat the Mexican Bean Beetle

—DANIELLE SHERRY

What It Looks Like:

The 16-spotted, light yellow to bronze-colored Mexican bean beetle *Epilachna varivestis* looks suspiciously like some of its ladybug relatives.

How It Harms Plants:

An adult beetle overwinters in leaf litter until it emerges in mid-spring, when warm days and rainfall trigger its appetite. A hungry adult beetle can live for two months, and waves of them will fly for miles looking for bean plants to eat. Feeding leads to mating, with each female laying about 750 eggs. The eggs hatch into spine-covered yellow larvae that feed on the underside of leaves until only a lacy leaf skeleton remains. The extensive defoliation can kill a plant.

How to Control It:

- Start by destroying its home. A fall sanitation program can deny shelter for beetles and reduce their numbers in spring.

- If possible, plant beans that the beetle does not like. Purple-podded varieties of snap beans, for instance, are more resistant than others.

- Protect young transplants with row covers.

- Crush any eggs you find, and handpick larvae and adults. Drop them into soapy water to kill them. Hope for hot weather or heavy rain, as these conditions will kill eggs and larvae.

Make Your Own Japanese Beetle Spray
—PAUL ZIMMERMAN

None of us like Japanese beetles, but the chemical alternatives can sometimes do more harm than good. Thankfully a natural control is here. It's simply a spray made from cedar oil—preferably Eastern Red Cedar. The principle is the same one used when storing sweaters in a cedar chest to keep moths away. When sprayed on roses it keeps the beetles away, and they fly off to another garden.

You can buy it from various online sites, but recently I found a recipe for it. Simply take a few red cedar planks, say a foot long each, and put them in a 1- or 2-gallon bucket. Pour hot water over it and let it steep like tea for 24 hours. Cut the planks in half if needed, but make sure they are totally immersed in the hot water.

Pour the liquid (don't dilute it) into the sprayer of your choice and spray the roses and the beetles. You may have to play around with how much cedar wood you use to get the right strength. When you have it right, the beetles will either fly away or drop off almost instantly.

I've also seen red cedar oil for sale by itself, and that diluted in water might also work.

Stop Wood Borers Before They Start
—JARET C. DANIELS

Healthy and vigorous plants are seldom attacked by wood-boring insects (some of the most destructive pests of ornamental trees and shrubs). Only plants that are stressed or weakened—by drought, heat, poor soil, or lack of proper nutrients—or plants that have been physically damaged are vulnerable to infestation. Keeping plants healthy and properly maintained is the best way to avoid infestation. If you think you have a borer problem, your best bet is to contact a professional nursery person or arborist. Proper identification is crucial and often difficult unless undertaken by a trained individual.

A wood-boring flower beetle

Milky White Foam on Stems and Leaves Equals Spittlebugs
—CHARLES W.G. SMITH

Spittlebugs look like leafhoppers and, like aphids and adelgids, use their piercing mouthparts to feed on plants by sucking out the sap. Each dollop of foam, a mix of slimy, sugary insect excretions and air bubbles, encloses a single spittlebug and protects it from desiccation and predators like lacewings and ladybugs. Most species are bright green, with big bulging eyes, though they can also be white, yellow, brown, or even pale orange.

Many species of spittlebug are common in North America. Each spittlebug species is most often host-specific, attacking a distinct plant or group of plants, such as holly, pine, strawberry, alfalfa, or juniper, as well as many herbaceous perennials and herbs. Spittlebug infestations are normally small, and the damage to mature plants is usually limited to yellow spots on the leaves. The foamy spittle usually appears from May to October in warm humid regions and for a few weeks around the summer solstice in more temperate climates.

You can control spittlebugs by handpicking them from the foam or by washing them off the plants with a strong spray of water. Adult spittlebugs (froghoppers) lay their eggs in weedy places and in plant stubble, where the eggs remain through winter. Extended control is often accomplished by keeping the area free of weeds and turning the soil to disturb egg-laying sites. Planting flowers such as alyssum (*Alyssum* spp. and cvs., Zones 4–9) to attract beneficial predatory insects like pirate bugs also helps.

Seal Your Home Against Stink Bugs
—GREG KRAWCYK

The brown marmorated stink bug (BMSB) has become a serious pest of all fruit, vegetable, and farm crops in the Mid-Atlantic region, and it will likely become a pest of these crops in other areas of the United States. In its native range of China, Japan, Korea, and Taiwan, it feeds on and can attack about 300 host plants, including apples, peaches, figs, mulberries, citrus, and persimmons.

Just under an inch long and brown on both its upper and lower body, it has the shield shape of other stink bugs but has lighter blue bands on the antennae and legs. It also has patches of coppery or bluish metallic punctures on its head.

The best way to stop its proliferation is to keep this stink bug from entering homes and buildings (where it overwinters). Cracks around windows, doors, siding, utility pipes, and chimneys and crevices underneath wood should be sealed with good-quality silicone or silicone-latex caulk. Damaged screens on doors and windows should be repaired or replaced. Exterior applications of insecticides may offer some minor relief from infestations. But spraying insecticides into cracks and crevices will not prevent the bug from emerging, so it is not a recommended treatment.

What's Infesting Your Bulbs?

—BECKY HEATH

Adult narcissus bulb flies (*Merodon equestris*) are about ⅓ inch long, with brownish bodies. They attack daffodils and other members of the *Amaryllis* family by laying eggs in the crown of host plants. The larvae, or maggots, hatch, work their way down into the bulb, and eat it, hollowing out the center and destroying the flower bud. Infested bulbs often rot or produce weak, yellowed, grasslike foliage.

If you suspect there might be a problem, dig up all of your daffodils in June, before the foliage dies. Immediately throw away any bulbs that are obviously infested and rotting. Store the remaining bulbs in a dry location with plenty of air circulation. At the end of summer, once again check each bulb for signs of the larvae; you may see a hole in the bulb, or it may have a very soft, hollow-feeling neck. There might also be a tiny white growth (about the size of a tooth) attached to the base of the bulb. Discard all bulbs with these symptoms because they probably contain the bulb fly larvae. Replant the healthy bulbs in fall, but continue to monitor them the following spring for signs of infestation.

Thwart Garlic Bloat Nematodes

—LYNN FELICI-GALLANT

In 2010, researchers from Cornell University discovered that nematodes were attacking the bulb and stem (bloat) of the garlic plant, causing as much as 80 to 90 percent crop loss in sections of one field in western New York. Infected plants exhibit stunting, yellowing and collapsing of older leaves, premature defoliation, and soft, shrunken, dark brown cloves that eventually crack and decay.

• Have the soil tested where you have planted, intend to plant, or have harvested garlic to determine the presence of bloat nematodes.

• Practice crop rotation. Do not plant anything in the garlic or onion family—or in other possible host crop families, including celery, parsley, and Shasta pea—in the same spot for four years. In the interim, plant cover crops, such as mustard, radish, and sorghum.

• Plant only nematode-free seeds. Request certified-clean seed from your seed source.

• Remove and destroy all plants if there is any evidence of nematodes. Dispose of all infected plants by burning them or by placing them in a sealed bag and throwing them away. Do not compost them.

Three Simple Steps to Remove Squash Vine Borers

—*FINE GARDENING* EDITORS

If you're noticing that the leaves of your squash plants are wilting despite plenty of water, chances are the dreaded squash vine borer has invaded the stems. Left unchecked, these pests can kill your plants. But never fear: All you need to do is perform a little squash-plant surgery to save your plants and preserve your harvest.

1. Follow the stem of the wilted leaves toward the base of the plant, and look for a perforation on the stem that looks like it's covered with bits of sawdust. This is the entry point of the insect.

2. Using a sharp knife, make an incision on the stem directly above the compromised spot. Gently peel the stem back to expose the small, white maggotlike borer. Remove the insect using the knife tip, and dispose of it by squishing it.

3. Bury the sliced section of the stem in the soil. The squash plant should recover completely and still set fruit over the following few weeks.

Squash vine borer (*Melittia cucurbitae*)

DEER

There are a number of strategies to deter browsing, from "deerproof" plants (see "Deer-Resistant Plants," p. 238) to electric fencing. They are most often effective when used with one another. But the most widely appealing method of control seems to be spray-on deer repellents. Commonly found in garden and home centers, these products are based on odor or taste or a combination of the two.

The effectiveness of repellents—or, for that matter, any deer-control method—depends on many factors: the number of deer browsing in your garden, the location of other preferred food sources, temperature, and snow cover (both duration and depth). The abundance and quality of grasses and forbs during the growing season and of mast (nuts of forest trees, such as acorns) in fall also influence the browsing behavior of deer.

—BRAD ROELLER

Odor-Based Repellents Send Up a Red Flag

These work because deer rely heavily on their sense of smell as their first warning against danger. Odor-based repellents contain strong-scented ingredients, like soap, putrefied eggs, garlic, bone tar, or the urine of a deer predator, like that of coyotes or bobcats. A number of odor-based repellents—such as soap sachets, processed sewage, mothballs, fabric-softener sheets, and blood meal—can be distributed around the area you wish to protect rather than sprayed on the plants.

Taste-Based Repellents Turn Deer Off

These products are usually sprayed on leaves to make a potential food source unpalatable. These repellents commonly include hot sauces, eggs, the fungicide thiram, and denatonium benzoate or Bitrex® (the bitter product added to many household items to deter young children from consuming them). Some of these repellents come in systemic forms, which are sprayed on a plant or added to the soil at planting time.

Repel Deer, Season by Season

Early Spring

Hang sachets filled with Milorganite® fertilizer around the area, or apply Milorganite (at half the recommended rate) around emerging bulbs and spring ephemerals. Reapply a month later. Applications of liquid foliar fertilizers/repellents, like Bobbex™, work well; just don't apply them in late summer or fall.

Late Spring/Summer

Apply spray repellents every three to four weeks once plants have fully leafed out. Spritz flower buds as they appear with an egg-based product, like Deer Off®; systemic products are not taken up by flower buds. Deer Stopper® is a good alternative.

- **Make your own repellent:** Mix and spray the following ingredients every 10 days: 1 egg, ⅓ cup whole milk, 1 tablespoon cooking oil, 1 tablespoon liquid soap, and 1 gallon water.

Late Summer/Fall

Continue your summer program. Evaluate environmental and biological factors (like the abundance of food sources or an increase in the deer population) to determine if you should rely on repellents or physical barriers, like fencing or burlap wraps, for the winter months.

Winter

Apply a blood-derived spray repellent, like Plantskydd®, during the dormant season (once in November and again in January). Odor- or taste-based repellents can be less effective in cold temperatures. Repellents containing thiram, like Bonide® Deer and Rabbit Repellent, will also work; just be sure to add an adhesive, like Vapor Gard®, because thiram does not withstand weather well.

DEER-RESISTANT PLANTS

If a fence is not practical, try plants that have a good track record against browsing deer. These include toxic plants (aconites, foxgloves, and daffodils), those with pungent foliage (alliums, bee balms, and catmints), and ferns and ornamental grasses.

Northeast

PEONIES

(*Paeonia* cvs.) please with color.

Zones: 3 to 8

Size: 2 to 4 feet tall and 2 to 3 feet wide

Conditions: Full sun; fertile, moisture-retentive soil. Plant with eyes no more than 2 inches deep.

Peonies come in colors from white to deepest red, including bicolors, and a wide range of single- and double-flower types. The large blooms, some fragrant, appear in late May or June. Foliage is glossy and often turns purplish in fall. Peonies make excellent cut flowers. Botrytis can be troublesome, however.

Peonies (*Paeonia* cvs.)

GIANT LAMBS' EARS

(*Stachys byzantina* 'Big Ears', syn. 'Countess Helen von Stein') edge out deer.

Zones: 4 to 8

Size: 6 inches tall and 12 to 15 inches wide

Conditions: Best in full sun and lean, dry soil

They form dense mats of felted, silvery leaves and make an excellent border edging. 'Big Ears' may tolerate winter wet better than other cultivars.

ASTILBES

(*Astilbe* spp. and cvs.) add backbone to a shady border.

Zones: 3 to 8

Size: 1 to 4 feet tall and 1 to 1½ feet wide

Conditions: Part to full shade; loamy, moist soil

They will tolerate some sun in the North with adequate moisture. For color, these perennials are the backbone of the summer shade garden. Their ferny foliage is topped with upright or arching plumes of white, pink, red, or lavender flowers. Through cultivar selection, it is possible to have floral display from June to September. Brunnera and pulmonarias are good companion plants.

GLOSSY-LEAVED PIERIS

(*Pieris japonica* and cvs.) provides year-round beauty.

Zones: 6 to 8

Size: 4 to 8 feet tall and 4 to 6 feet wide

Conditions: Partial shade; moist, acidic, well-drained soil amended with organic matter

Pieris, often mistakenly called andromeda, is an upright, evergreen shrub with glossy leaves. The reddish new foliage is a bonus. Fragrant flower panicles of creamy white or pink appear in April. Use it in a shrub border or in transition plantings from a garden setting to the woodlands.

JAPANESE SPIREA

(*Spiraea japonica* 'Little Princess') is great for beds and foundations.

Zones: 4 to 9

Size: 3 feet tall and 3 feet wide

Conditions: Full sun; any well-drained soil

'Little Princess' forms a tidy mound, topped in June with flat rosy pink flowers. It may repeat bloom, especially if spent flowers are removed. Foliage often turns bronzy purple in fall. The shrub works well in foundation plantings or in a mixed border with perennials.

—MARY ANN McGOURTY

South

NEW YORK FERN

(*Thelypteris noveboracensis*) spreads out in shady spots.

Zones: 2 to 8

Size: 18 inches high

Conditions: Light shade; moist, well-drained soil

Like many other ferns, this plant is not appetizing to deer. This strong, upright grower spreads aggressively by long, creeping rhizomes, making excellent naturalized sweeps in the woodland where plenty of space is available.

HARDY SUGARCANE

(*Saccharum arundinaceum*) does double duty.

Zones: 6 to 10

Size: 9 feet high and 12 feet wide

Conditions: Full sun; any soil

All ornamental grasses are reputed to be deer resistant. This gorgeous one could also form a hedge to keep deer out. When it's at its peak in late summer, people regularly knock on my door to request the name. The huge blooms of delicate pink panicles eventually fade to silver. But the sharp-edged, gray-green leaves give a mean paper cut, and it's a chore to transplant.

'SIX HILLS GIANT' CATMINT

(*Nepeta* 'Six Hills Giant') has foliage deer hate.

Zones: 3 to 8

Size: 30 inches high and 2 feet wide

New York fern (*Thelypteris noveboracensis*)

Conditions: Prefers full sun and well-drained soil but tolerates partial shade and average soil

This catmint does not just deter deer but actually repels them with its aromatic foliage. It offers a mound of silvery, fine-textured foliage and lavender-blue flowers that bloom from June until frost.

WHITE FLORIDA ANISE

(*Illicium floridanum f. album*) is a shrub for full shade.

Zones: 7 to 9

Size: 8 feet high by 8 feet wide

Conditions: Partial sun to shade; tolerates wet soil

This native, evergreen, white-flowering shrub has long, shiny leaves with the fragrance of anise when crushed. It is unusual in that it remains dense even in full shade, and its late-spring flowers are a beautiful star shape. It can be pruned into a hedge or small tree.

'ARP' ROSEMARY

(*Rosmarinus officinalis* 'Arp') is tasty.

Zones: 7 to 11

Size: 4 feet high and 8 feet wide

Conditions: Full sun; well-drained soil

This classic garden plant is evergreen and edible. 'Arp' has light blue flowers and is most attractive if trimmed regularly. It's also hardier and spreads wider than most other cultivars.

—AMY FAHMY

Midwest

RUGOSA ROSES
(*Rosa* cvs.) make a good hedge.

Zones: 2 to 9

Size: Up to 6 feet tall and 4 feet wide

Conditions: Full sun; well-amended soil

Mixed with redtwig dogwoods and old cotoneaster bushes, rugosa roses thrive in a hedge that screens my neighbor's garage and driveway from our view. Deer don't bother the wrinkled leaves, fragrant flowers, or bristled stems of rugosa roses. I usually harvest the edible red-orange hips before winter arrives.

ALLIUMS
(*Allium* spp. and cvs.) act as floral "guard dogs."

Zones: 3 to 11

Size: Varies by species from 4 inches to 6 feet tall

Conditions: Sun or shade; well-drained soil

These ornamental relatives of garlic and onions make attractive "guard dogs" in my front-yard beds. I keep planting new alliums so that one or another is in bloom nearly all summer. When these bulbs multiply, as *A. moly* does, they are easy to transplant.

SCENTED CRANESBILL
(*Geranium macrorrhizum* and cvs.) can cover a lot of ground.

Zones: 4 to 8

Size: 20 inches tall and 2 feet wide

Conditions: Partial shade; well-drained soil

I dislike this plant's odor, so I suspect that it's one of the main deer deterrents in my garden. But I appreciate scented cranesbill's attractive, toothy leaves and small flowers of purple, pink, or white. It makes a great ground cover under a honeylocust tree, where it conceals dying daffodil foliage and serves as a foil for hostas and grasses. Cranesbills are easy to transplant because their roots grow close to the soil's surface.

WILLOW BLUE-STAR
(*Amsonia tabernaemontana*) holds its own all season.

Zones: 3 to 9

Size: 2 to 3 feet tall and 18 inches wide

Conditions: Full sun to partial shade; well-drained soil

In addition to willow blue-star's small but charming clusters of blue flowers in late spring, it has upright, willowlike leaves that turn clear yellow in fall. It easily tops 3 feet in a moist spot in my shady backyard, but it remains closer to 2 feet tall in a drier, front-yard bed.

SILVERY LUNGWORTS
(*Pulmonaria* spp. and cvs.) fend off deer.

Zones: 2 to 8

Size: 6 to 18 inches wide and 18 to 36 inches tall

Conditions: Full sun to partial shade; fertile, moist soil

Lungwort species and cultivars offer silver-spotted or silver-splashed leaves in the shadiest areas, along with the bonus of delicate spring flowers of blue, pink, or white. Their leaves hide daffodil foliage as it yellows. If lungworts are not watered during drought, they go dormant and reappear the following spring.

—MARYALICE KOEHNE

Lower Plains

MILKWEED
(*Asclepias tuberosa*) feeds butterflies, not deer.

Zones: 4 to 9

Size: 36 inches tall and 12 inches wide

Conditions: Full sun; rich, well-drained soil

The recognizable orange flowers of this milkweed species appear in early summer and are followed by narrow green seedpods with silky white hairs. Butterflies love to sip the flower nectar, while monarch caterpillars feed on the foliage. Also try the cultivars 'Hello Yellow' (yellow) and 'Gay Butterflies' (red, orange, and yellow mixed) in combination with other prairie plants and wildflowers.

Milkweed (*Asclepias tuberosa*)

SALVIAS

(*Salvia* spp. and cvs.) serve up spiky summer blooms.

Zones: 5 to 11

Size: 12 to 36 inches tall and wide

Conditions: Full sun; medium-to-dry, well-drained soil—no heavy clay

There are many great salvias to choose from. Cultivated varieties like *Salvia × sylvestris* 'Blue Hill' (blue), 'May Night' (violet), and 'Rose Queen' (pink) offer attractive flower spikes atop clean, deep green foliage in summer. Our native species also put on quite a show later in the season. *Salvia azurea* has powder blue flowers, while our southern belle, *S. greggii*, seems to have an almost endless color palette.

CONEFLOWERS

(*Echinacea* spp. and cvs.) offer new, vibrant colors.

Zones: 3 to 9

Size: 18 to 48 inches tall and wide

Conditions: Full sun; well-drained soil

Vibrant and bold, new *Echinacea* hybrids have turned the perennial world upside down. Orange-flowering 'Art's Pride' and yellow-flowering 'Mango Meadowbrite' stand out against dark green foliage on upright stems. Of course, the native species *E. pallida* and *E. angustifolia* are nothing to shake a stick at, and they also are not troubled by deer.

APACHE PLUME

(*Fallugia paradoxa*) thrives in tough sites.

Zones: 5 to 10

Size: 4 feet tall and wide

Conditions: Full sun; medium-to-dry, well-drained soil

One of the showiest of our native shrubs, this plant is everblooming with white flowers followed by pink, silky, plumed seed heads. It can take a few years before Apache plume will bloom prolifically, but it tolerates harsh southern exposures. It makes a great specimen plant.

COLUMBINES

(*Aquilegia canadensis* and cvs.) add a touch of elegance.

Zones: 3 to 8

Size: 12 to 24 inches tall and wide

Conditions: Full sun or partial shade; fertile, well-drained soil

Canada columbine is a native plant popular among gardeners and nonthreatening wildlife alike. Butterflies and hummingbirds flock in spring to its yellow flowers with red spurs. Noteworthy selections include 'Canyon Vista', a dwarf with dark red spurs, and a yellow form called 'Corbett'.

—SCOTT VOGT

Rocky Mountains

BEARDED IRISES

(*Iris* cvs.) are a must-have.

Zones: 3 to 9

Size: 6 inches to 4 feet tall and 1 to 2 feet wide

Conditions: Full sun; good drainage; tolerates drought and abuse. Most like to be divided after three to four years.

The range here is nearly endless, from dwarf types to flamboyant giants. Though they look and smell good enough to eat, deer seem to avoid them. The plants' forgiving nature and strappy leaves make them indispensable to many gardeners.

Bearded iris (*Iris* cvs.)

SUNSET HYSSOP

(*Agastache rupestris*) has a scent that humans like and deer hate.

Zones: 4 to 9

Size: 2 feet tall and wide

Conditions: Not finicky about soil, but full sun and good drainage are essential. Regular but infrequent watering will keep it at its best.

Most hyssops have pungent leaves, and several species and cultivars are commonly available.

SHRUBBY CLEMATIS

(*Clematis integrifolia*) makes for a nice change.

Zones: 4 to 11

Size: Nonclimbing type to 3 feet tall and wide

Conditions: Full sun to partial shade; average garden soil and regular watering

Most clematis seem to be resistant to deer. Try this semi-shrubby perennial for a different effect in a mixed border. Nodding midsummer blooms are urn-shaped in shades of pink and blue.

RUSSIAN SAGE

(*Perovskia atriplicifolia* and cvs.) is a stalwart in all aspects.

Zones: 6 to 9

Size: 4 feet tall and 5 feet wide

Conditions: Full sun; well-drained soil; drought tolerant

These pungent shrubs are well known for their lavender blooms in mid- to late summer. Dissected sage green leaves blend well in western landscapes and have a powerful fragrance when brushed.

LEAD PLANT

(*Amorpha canescens*) is a native that withstands browsing.

Zones: 2 to 8

Size: 3 feet tall and up to 5 feet wide

Conditions: Full sun; any well-drained soil

This shrub is a tough prairie native that withstands drought once established. Luminous purple flower spikes with a dusting of orange are produced in midsummer.

—DAN JOHNSON

Winter daphne (*Daphne odora*)

Northwest

WINTER DAPHNE

(*Daphne odora*) is an early charmer.

Zones: 7 to 9

Size: 4 feet tall and wide

Conditions: Filtered shade; slightly alkaline to slightly acidic soil that is rich in humus. Give it heavy pruning to keep it bushy.

Winter daphne is a fabulous woody plant that blooms in February, when every promise of spring is cherished. The small pink flowers are exotically fragrant. The waxy, lightly margined leaves are evergreen.

HELLEBORES

(*Helleborus* spp. and cvs.) offer an array of colors.

Zones: 4 to 9

Size: 1 to 1½ feet tall and wide; some can reach 4 feet tall by 2 feet wide

Conditions: Filtered shade; woodsy, humus-rich soil

Also called Lenten roses and Christmas roses because of their extremely early bloom periods, hellebores are not roses at all—good news for gardeners in deer country.

MONKSHOOD

(*Aconitum* spp. and cvs.) steps in for delphinium.

Zones: 3 to 8

Size: 2 to 10 feet tall and 1 to 1½ feet wide

Conditions: Partial shade; moist, fertile soil

For those who desperately want delphiniums (a deer delicacy), monkshoods are a terrific substitute. They come in shades of blue, purple, yellow, and cream on tall spires.

DEER FERN

(*Blechnum spicant*) adds texture and intrigue.

Zones: 5 to 8

Size: 8 to 20 inches tall and 24 inches wide

Conditions: Partial to deep shade; moist, acidic soil

Deer ferns have sterile and fertile fronds, which look quite different from one another. While the sterile fronds lie flat to the ground and are broad, the fertile fronds stand straight up and are narrow.

LILYTURF

(*Liriope* spp. and cvs.) shows off in the shade.

Zones: 6 to 10

Size: 10 to 12 inches tall and 12 to 18 inches wide

Conditions: Partial to full shade; light, acidic soil. Protect it from strong winds.

Recent introductions have been taking lilyturf out of the shadows and into the spotlight. *Liriope muscari* 'Silver Dragon' (Zones 6–10) is a breathtaking, iridescent beauty. A shimmering silver stripe runs down the arching blades.

—CINDEE EICHENGREEN

West

'CORONATION GOLD' YARROW

(*Achillea* 'Coronation Gold') doesn't mind drought.

Zones: 3 to 9

Size: 3 feet tall and 2 feet wide

Conditions: Full sun; well-drained soil

This perennial's fernlike, scented, gray-green leaves are topped with flat yellow flowers. It's drought tolerant and has a long bloom season, beginning in early summer. Cut the foliage and old flower stalks to the ground every year. It combines well with lavender.

EVERGREEN CURRANT

(*Ribes viburnifolium*) attracts birds.

Zones: 9 to 10

Size: 4 feet tall and 12 feet wide

Conditions: Dry shade; average soil

This California native can root wherever the red stems touch the ground. When brushed, the bright green leaves give off a pleasing, viburnum-like scent. It bears tiny clusters of maroon flowers in spring and berries in fall.

'Coronation Gold' yarrow (*Achillea* 'Coronation Gold')

ENGLISH LAVENDER

(*Lavandula angustifolia* and cvs.) is a good choice.

Zones: 5 to 8

Size: 3 feet tall and wide

Conditions: Full sun; well-drained soil

English lavender's silvery gray, aromatic foliage is topped in summer with lavender-blue to dark purple flowers on long stems. All of the many selections are wonderful, but this plant needs good drainage; more lavender is killed by overwatering than anything else.

LAVENDER COTTON

(*Santolina chamaecyparissus* and cvs.) makes an attractive edge.

Zones: 6 to 9

Size: 2 feet high and wide

Conditions: Full sun; average soil

This gray shrub has fine-textured, mound-forming foliage. Yellow, buttonlike flowers appear in summer. Great in Mediterranean gardens, it needs cutting back every year or it becomes long and woody. It is wonderful for edging, too.

'POWIS CASTLE' ARTEMISIA

(*Artemisia* 'Powis Castle') likes room to grow.

Zones: 7 to 9

Size: 3 feet tall and an indeterminate spread

Conditions: Full sun; well-drained soil

This plant has scented, silver filigree foliage. It can colonize an area by rooting where stems touch the ground. Mine has filled a 20-foot-long by 10-foot-wide border. Beautiful in full sun, it needs average water or its leaves will look droopy in the height of summer.

—PAT RUBIN

RABBITS, MOLES, VOLES, AND OTHER CRITTERS

Recognize Rabbit Damage
—HELGA OLKOWSKI

If you walk out into your garden one morning and notice that it looks like someone took pruning shears and snipped off the stems of young plants with clean, angled cuts; mowed your lettuces and beet foliage to the ground; or gnawed rings around the trunks of trees or vines, extending upward about 2½ feet, your garden has likely been visited by a rabbit or two. To confirm your suspicions, look around for the ubiquitous ¼- to ½-inch-round fecal pellets that rabbits seem to drop constantly. The presence of their footprints, consisting of an alternating pattern of small front feet and large back feet, is another clue to the identity of the culprits.

Fences Are the Most Humane (and Labor-Intensive) Solution
—HELGA OLKOWSKI

Preventing rabbits' access to your plants is the most humane solution to the dilemma of these unwanted foragers. Cottontails will not jump a 2-foot-high fence, so constructing a simple fence of wire mesh (with mesh no larger than 1 inch square), 30 to 36 inches high, is an almost foolproof method of protection. The lower end of the wire mesh should be turned outward at a 90-degree angle and buried 6 inches in the ground to discourage rabbits from digging under the fence. You can also use regular 20-gauge poultry netting supported by stakes.

Nets May Keep Bunnies at Bay
—DORRIS OLSON

I grow perennials from seed, and the small plants are a favorite lunch for hungry rabbits. My effective, no-cost solution is to use plastic mesh produce bags (the kind that onions come in) to cover the young plants.

I push three or four small wooden stakes or twigs into the soil around the plants. Then I slip the produce bag over the stakes, which will hold the bag upright. The rabbits do not chew through the plastic, and the plants are protected while getting light and air.

A SIMPLE NET

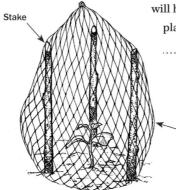

Stake

Mesh produce bag

Know Your Moles From Your Voles

—JESSICA WALLISER

Mole

The Mole

- Protruding pink snout
- Outward-facing, stubby front claws
- 6 to 8 inches long
- Smooth, dark brown to black fur

Diet: Moles are insectivores. Their prey includes earthworms, slugs, grubs, and other underground insects.

Damage: Moles live underground, usually alone or in pairs during mating season. In spring and early summer, you'll see their raised tunnels throughout your garden and lawn; they also create mounds of excavated dirt. In summer and fall, their tunnels are deeper, so you're unlikely to notice any damage.

The Vole

- Small ears
- Elongated snout
- Short tail
- 4 to 6 inches long
- Light to dark brown or gray fur

Diet: Voles are herbivores. They eat roots, bulbs, tree bark, and tubers.

Damage: Voles are often noticed in early spring after snowmelt, when their well-worn traveling paths are present on top of the soil and lawn. Unlike moles, they devour plant roots. You may also notice quarter-size burrow entrances. Voles live in colonies and are active year-round, day and night.

What to do about them: The damage moles cause is purely aesthetic, so it's often fine just to let them be. Press down their tunnels, and overseed with grass, if necessary. Voles can be trapped with mousetraps: Bait them with peanut butter, and place them across the animals' paths. There are also several repellents that deter both moles and voles. The odor and taste of liquid or granular castor oil–based products help keep these critters out of the garden; many also deter gophers and armadillos.

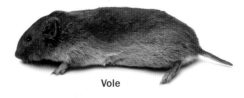

Vole

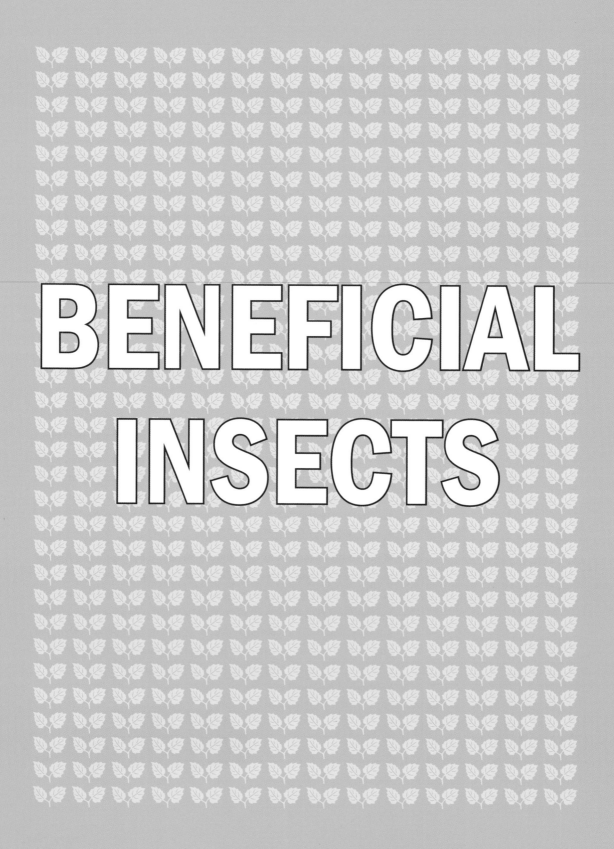

BENEFICIAL INSECTS

BIRDS, BEES, BATS & BEETLES

To create a welcoming habitat for your insect helpers, first you need to know something about them. A good way to start is to grab a hand lens and a picture book of insects and take a rough census of your resident population. If you've avoided using pesticides and have a variety of plants growing, you may find many allies already present. The ones you're most likely to see include lady beetles, ground beetles, lacewings, hover flies, a couple of true bugs, and a few tiny wasps. These can be divided into two groups: those that eat their prey directly (predators) and those that deposit their eggs on or into their host (parasitoids).

—JOE QUEIROLO

Meet the Beetles
—JOE QUEIROLO

The two kinds of beetle that are most helpful are lady beetles (aka ladybugs) and ground beetles, both predators.

Lady beetles prey on aphids and other soft-bodied insects. The adults will eat as many as 50 aphids per day. If you have enough aphids, and the beetles stick around long enough to lay eggs, each hatched larva will eat some 400 aphids before entering its pupal stage. There are many species of lady beetle that attack many different kinds of prey. The adults are independent, flighty creatures. If you buy some at the garden center and release them into your garden, be prepared to watch most of them fly away to your neighbor's yard. Those that stay, though, will be a big help.

Ground beetles don't fly much, preferring to run away when disturbed. You probably won't see them unless you uncover their hiding places. If I see them at all, it's when I'm picking up old piles of weeds. They're relatively large (about ¾ inch) and dark, with long, jointed legs. They're nocturnal hunters, rooting among leaf litter for insect eggs and larvae.

Hang egg cases, cards, and tapes

To hang an egg case, securely fasten a piece of wire, twine, or fishing line around it, threading it with a needle right through the case, if possible. Tie it to a branch or a plant 3 to 4 feet off the ground in a sheltered location hidden by foliage. Some beneficial insect adults or eggs are secured to perforated cards that can be torn apart and attached to the branches or foliage of the infested plants. Others come attached to a tape that can be wound around the branches of a plant. Those released in cases, on cards, or on tape include:

- Praying mantis
- Spined soldier bugs
- Trichogramma wasps

Sprinkle bugs evenly

Many beneficial insects will arrive as active, mobile immature insects or adults ready for immediate release. Place a small number of them (up to 10, depending on the pest density) on an infested plant. Be sure to distribute them evenly throughout the garden. Insects released this way include:

- Aphid parasites
- Green lacewings
- Lady beetles
- Leaf miner parasites
- Mealybug destroyers
- Mealybug parasite
- Minute pirate bugs

Broadcast granulated materials

Some beneficials arrive in containers mixed with a material like rice hulls, bran hulls, or vermiculite to keep them separated and to help disperse them evenly. Sprinkle a small amount of the mixture onto infested plants, distributing it evenly over the targeted garden space. Those released this way include:

- Aphid predators
- Grasshopper pathogen
- Green lacewing eggs
- Predatory mites
- Spined soldier bugs
- Thrips predators

Spray solutions onto plants or soil

Some beneficial insects come in a powder or as a liquid concentrate that must be mixed with water according to the package directions and applied with a watering can, hose applicator, or a pump sprayer. Be sure to treat the entire space evenly. If you are applying the solution to soil or lawn, water the ground thoroughly before you apply the solution, then keep it moist for the next two weeks. Treatments applied this way include:

- Beneficial nematodes
- Bt (*Bacillus thuringiensis*)

Dust milky spore powder on infested areas

Some beneficial organisms, like milky spore, a bacterium used to control Japanese beetle grubs, come as powders. To treat a target area, apply 1 level teaspoon of milky spore powder on the turf surface about every 3 feet in a grid pattern to ensure that the entire area is effectively inoculated. Water the treated area for 15 to 30 minutes after you have finished applying the powder.

Place Bt dunks in water

Bt (*Bacillus thuringiensis*) is a naturally occurring bacterium that affects various insects, including two bothersome pests, mosquitoes and black flies. It is sold as cakes, or dunks, which resemble hard doughnuts. It is nontoxic to humans, pets, birds, fish, plants, beneficial insects, and wildlife and can be used in ornamental ponds. To use, simply place individual dunks in areas of standing water where mosquitoes and black flies typically breed. One dunk usually covers about 100 square feet and lasts for four weeks. As the dunk dissolves, the Bt is slowly released into the water, killing the developing larvae.

Bees
—PAM BAGGETT

Bring the Buzz Back to Your Garden

With the honeybee population being decimated by parasitic mites, other pollinators, like bumblebees, provide an underappreciated service we can no longer take for granted. Bumblebees are drawn to flowers by sight and by smell, and recent research indicates that they have internal compasses that guide them back to choice feeding sites. The bumblebees that frequent my gardens are especially fond of flowers on spikes—like salvia and lavender—but they also feed on nectar and collect pollen from daisy-type flowers like zinnias. In addition to flower shapes, masses of brightly colored blooms attract bumblebees better than individual flowers. Many of the flowers they choose in my garden are blue, purple, or white, but I don't discount orange, yellow, and red. Most bright colors will do the job. Last, bumblebee-attracting flowers must be stable enough to support the weight of these pollinators.

Best for Bumblebees
Spring

• Chinese forget-me-not (*Cynoglossum amabile*)

Summer

• Anise hyssop (*Agastache foeniculum*)

• Lavender (*Lavandula* × *intermedia*)

• Wand flower (*Gaura lindheimeri*)

• Calamint (*Calamintha nepeta*)

• Joe Pye weed (*Eupatorium purpureum*) (butterflies love it, too)

• Spiderwort (*Tradescantia virginica* 'Zwanenburg Blue')

• 'Hella Lacy' New England Aster (*Aster novae-angliae* 'Hela Lacy')

Autumn

• Goldenrod (*Solidago rugosa* 'Fireworks')

Bumblebees are great pollinators.

Forget Chickens! Let Guinea Fowl Eat the Pests

—JEANNETTE FERGUSON

Guinea fowl

Prior to keeping guinea fowl, I raised chickens and a few ducks, but they caused as many problems as they solved. When left to range, chickens will scratch for food under the surface, uprooting grass, flowers, or whatever is in their way, and so they are not always helpful gardeners. Ducks are fun, but their droppings are messy, so I no longer keep them.

Guinea fowl pick bugs from within their reach and normally will not scratch for food. They patrol our property in groups, pecking at insects with every step they take. It is not uncommon to observe them following the riding mower, grabbing bugs stirred up by its cutting blades.

Great little garden helpers, guinea fowl also eat weeds and weed seeds. Their diet should be supplemented with millet and vegetable greens. Be careful what scraps you feed them, however; once guinea fowl acquire a taste for a particular crop, they will continue to favor it while ranging in the garden.

Their droppings, a rich source of beneficial nitrogen for our lawn, are dry and quickly disappear. In addition, guinea fowl are great watch birds, loudly screeching at anything new or strange that enters the garden, such as predators or other uninvited guests.

Butterflies Prefer Nature to a Butterfly House

—JARET C. DANIELS

Designed to provide shelter for hibernating adult butterflies from inclement weather or cold temperatures, butterfly houses have become familiar garden accessories. These structures resemble birdhouses, but they are equipped with elongated slits instead of round holes for entry. Most have a hinged door or removable lid so that bits of branches or twigs can be added for adult butterflies to wedge between or grab hold of.

While the premise sounds believable, gardeners become perplexed when they fail to see any butterflies actively occupying these cozy homes. In reality, butterfly houses aren't effective at attracting butterflies to a garden. And even if they did work, butterflies would not come knocking during the summer.

Although there are a number of butterfly species, like the mourning cloak (*Nymphalis antiopa*), that survive the winter months as adults, even in cold northern climates, they prefer to hibernate in the old-fashioned places: under bark, in vegetation, or in a brush pile. To a butterfly, these natural areas are more inviting and protective than an artificial structure placed out in the open.

RULES TO GARDEN BY

10 Ways to Keep Your Garden Healthy

—A. R. CHASE

1. Examine plants carefully before buying. Don't take home a plant with dead spots, rotted stems, or insects. These problems can easily spread to your healthy plants and are sometimes hard to get rid of once established.

In addition to checking the tops of plants, always inspect the root quality. One does not often see customers doing this in a garden center, but it should be a common sight. Place your hand on the soil surface with the plant stem between your fingers. Gently invert the pot and shake the plant loose. You may have to tap the edge of the pot against a solid surface to loosen the roots from the pot. Roots should be firm, usually white, and spaced all over the root ball. Dark or mushy roots are not a good sign. Even when the tops appear healthy, it's just a matter of time before a rotted root system kills a plant.

2. Use fully composted yard waste. Not all materials in a compost pile decompose at the same rate. Some materials may have degraded sufficiently to be put in the garden, while others have not. Thorough composting generates high temperatures for extended lengths of time, which actually kill any pathogens in the material. Infected plant debris that has not undergone this process will reintroduce potential diseases into your garden. If you are not sure of the conditions of your compost pile, you should avoid using yard waste as mulch under sensitive plants and avoid including possibly infected debris in your pile.

3. Keep an eye on your bugs. Insect damage to plants is much more than cosmetic. Viruses and bacteria often can only enter a plant through some sort of opening, and bug damage provides that. Some insects actually act as a transport for viruses, spreading them from one plant to the next. Aphids are one of the most common carriers, and thrips spread impatiens necrotic spot virus, which has become a serious problem for commercial producers over the past 10 years. Insect attacks are another way to put a plant under stress, rendering it less likely to fend off disease.

4. Clean up in the fall. It is always best to clean out the garden in the fall, even if you live in a moderate climate. This is not only an effective deterrent to disease but also a good way to control diseases already in your garden.